God Girl

God Girl

Becoming the Woman You're Meant to Be

Hayley DiMarco

Revell

a division of Baker Publishing Group
Grand Rapids, Michigan

Hungry
Planet

© 2009 by Hungry Planet
Published by Revell
a division of Baker Publishing Group
P.O. Box 6287, Grand Rapids, MI 49516-6287
www.revellbooks.com

Printed in the United States of America

Library of Congress Cataloging-in-Publication Data
DiMarco, Hayley.
     God girl : becoming the woman you're meant to be / Hayley DiMarco.
          p.   cm.
     ISBN 978-0-8007-1940-1 (pbk.)
     1. Teenage girls—Conduct of life. 2. Teenage girls—Religious life. I. Title.
BJ1681.D565 2009
248.8'33—dc22   2009026729

Published in association with Yates & Yates, LLP, Literary Agents, Orange, California.

Creative direction by Hungry Planet
Interior design by Sarah Lowrey Brammeier

     11   12   13   14   15   16   9 8 7 6

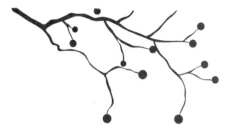

Contents

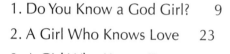

"Live in me,

and I will live in you.

A branch cannot produce

any fruit by itself.

It has to stay attached
to the vine.

In the same way, you cannot

produce fruit unless

you live in me."

—John 15:4

1

Do You Know a God Girl?

I believe that the God Girl is the most amazing girl on earth.

That's because she worships the one true God, Jehovah. Yahweh. The Alpha and the Omega. The Beginning and the End. Everything she does is colored by the fact that **she loves her God with all her heart, all her soul, all her mind, and all her strength.** She knows where she came from and where she is going. Her life isn't perfect; it wasn't meant to be. It's sometimes messy, sometimes loud, and sometimes uncomfortable. She has dreams, hopes, prayers. She wants what every other girl wants: to love and to be loved. She wants acceptance and laughter. She wants hope and peace. Some days she is on top of the world and nothing can bring her down, and some days she is certain she has hit bottom. But what makes the God Girl different from just any girl is the God in her name. Her right relationship with the Creator of the universe. Her acknowledgment that she can't do this messed-up and crazy life on her own and her willingness to

trust the God who can. When life is more than she can bear, God is more than she needs.

The life of the God Girl centers around not what others think of her or do to her but who he is. She defines her life by the fact that she belongs to him. The most pivotal moment in her life was the moment she said yes to his call. When she heard him say "I love you" and she believed it. When Jesus reached out of the pages of that old Bible, grabbed her hand, and said, "Come with me. Make me Lord of your life, and I will be with you always. You will never have to fear again."

Do you remember that invitation? Did you say yes?

I remember when I did.

I had been searching so long for him. I went to a Catholic high school, and there I learned a lot about God's holiness and wrath. But most of all I learned that I was broken, messed up, weak, and imperfect. The God I saw could not accept me—I was too dirty, too unlovable. But I wanted him desperately. I knew that if I could just get to him, he would fix me, love me, heal me. And so every weekend I turned on the TV and watched an old preacher named Jimmy Swaggart. And every week I cried and accepted

Christ into my heart. *Every week.* It just never seemed to stick.

By the time I was in college, I was certain of only one thing: I was not good enough for God. I was driving limousines at night and going to TV and movie auditions during the day. And then I met him. His name was Greg, he was so cute, and I wanted him to want me.

And so I pursued him. He drove limousines too, and he was a Christian. I told him I was too, though I didn't know what that really meant. Then one day he took a risk. He asked me why, if I was a Christian, I talked like a sailor. You see, I loved cussing. I had a potty mouth.

I thought about it for a minute, and then I told him, "I decided a long time ago that I wasn't good enough for God, and I know I'm going to hell. I just can't do everything he asks. So I figure if I'm going to hell, I might as well have fun on the way."

Greg looked at me with such confusion. And then he said the most important words I'd heard in my life: "You realize that once you are saved, you are always saved, don't you?"

"Where did you hear that?" I said in shock.

"It's right here," he said as he pointed to his old, worn Bible. He opened it up to Romans 10:9 and read these words: "If you confess with your mouth, 'Jesus is Lord,' and believe in your heart that God raised him from the dead, you will be saved" (NIV).

I remember this so vividly. I stood up with both hands on my hips and yelled, "Why hasn't anyone ever told me this?"

> If you confess with your mouth, 'Jesus is Lord,' and believe in your heart that God raised him from the dead, you will be saved.
>
> Romans 10:9 NIV

This whole time Jesus was right there for me, and I didn't see him. I couldn't believe how close he was. How permanent and secure. So suddenly my life changed. In an instant it was like the light went on and I saw things I never saw before. Greg gave me that Bible, and it sits beside me now, even as I write these words. I read it that day, and over the next month I read the entire thing. I was in awe! I was amazed that the answers to every question I had about life were right there in that book I had looked at so many times before and not understood a word of. It was as if a veil had been lifted, and suddenly it all made sense to me.

From that point on I made it my mission to help people find the Jesus who meets all their needs as he met mine. The power of salvation was so strong in my life that I knew it would change anyone's life who would just listen. My life didn't change completely in one day, or even in one month, but as I began to make his Word a part of my life, the layers of mess started to peel off of me. And now I am a completely new creature.

God changes lives. There is no question. If he hasn't changed yours, it's only because you haven't let him. It can be scary to let him and easy to believe that he won't come through, or that if you trust him you'll be fooled. But I'm living proof: that isn't true. He was there all along; I just didn't have the facts.

God Girl is my gift to your heart. I pray that it will be a window into his Word and a lifeline to your soul. If you believe that Jesus is who he says he is, then you, my brave heart, are a God Girl. You might not feel like one right now, but you shall. Trust that you were led here for a reason. Trust *your* purpose and dive into the life of a God Girl. You won't be disappointed.

The truth is that if you are a God Girl it is because of who you worship, not who you are, or what you've done or failed to do.

Searching for More

The truth is that if you are a God Girl, it is because of who you worship, not who you are or what you've done or failed to do. His reaching out and choosing you changed who you are at the very core. You might not feel it every day, but trust me when I say that it did.

Deep down inside you might feel like you've failed to love him as deeply as you should. You have had so many missed opportunities, made so many wrong decisions. Sure, you're a good girl—you haven't turned your back on him or tried to be bad; you're just human and sinful.

And you know you want more.

You want more of him,

more of the real you,

more faith.

It's true, you know, that "there is no one righteous, not even one" (Romans 3:10 NIV). So it should be no surprise that your life isn't exactly what you pictured. And it's good that you want more, because more is exactly what is in store for you when you take a fearless look at God's Word and are willing to let it reveal all your bruises, cuts, bumps, and blemishes. When you let it expose the very center of your beating heart with all its selfish motives and unmet needs, all its hopes and

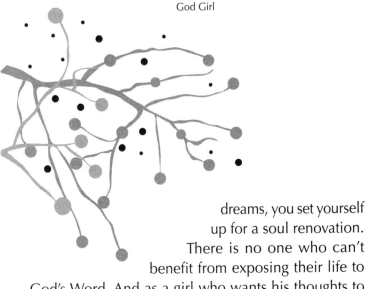

dreams, you set yourself up for a soul renovation. There is no one who can't benefit from exposing their life to God's Word. And as a girl who wants his thoughts to be your very own, you cannot fail to open up Scripture and be changed. The only question is, how much change are you willing to go for?

Do you want more of God in your life? More of his love, more of his peace, more of his presence? Then hold still and hang on, because that's just what's in store for you. Your natural human tendency is to move, to wander, and to squirm. Staying, or abiding, is often one of the hardest things, but it's the thing that brings the very Christ in whom you abide deeper into your life.

Being the Branch

I want you to imagine a branch, and this branch isn't attached to anything. Not to a tree or a vine. It is connected to nothing bigger than itself.

16

Can you see it? Lying there all alone?

How long do you think that branch will remain flexible and grow leaves or even fruit? How long until it gets brittle and snaps under the weight of someone's foot?

Remember how I said that before I became a God Girl I had wanted God to heal me but didn't think I deserved his love? Well, I was that branch—alone, without anything or anyone bigger than myself—until I realized that I needed to be attached to something stronger, something that would feed me spiritually and emotionally.

Jesus, in the book of John, describes us as branches, but he also describes himself as the vine. And he promises us that if we are willing to remain in him (in other words, stay attached to that something bigger), then we will have everything good to show from it. In Galatians, the good—the stuff that grows from a healthy branch that stays attached to the vine—is called fruit. And in human terms it's stuff like this: love, joy, peace, patience, kindness, goodness, faithfulness, gentleness, and self-control (see Galatians 5:22–23). It's you at your best. It's everything you think and do that is good. And it's all the stuff that brings glory to God and makes him look amazing in the eyes of others. It's the cool part of your life, and God's main goal is to bring that stuff out of you.

So let's take a quick look at the entire verse about the vine and the branches, shall we? Just to help it sink in as you read, do this. Put a cross above all the words that stand for Jesus (like *vine, I,* etc.). And draw a cloud around all the words that refer to the Father (like *vinedresser, he,* etc.). Then underline all the action words (like *removes, prunes,* etc.).

[Then Jesus said,] "I am the true vine, and my Father takes care of the vineyard. He removes every one of my branches that doesn't produce fruit. He also prunes every branch that does produce fruit to make it produce more fruit. You are already clean because of what I have told you. Live in me, and I will live in you. A branch cannot produce any fruit by itself. It has to stay attached to the vine. In the same way, you cannot produce fruit unless you live in me. I am the vine. You are the branches. Those who live in me while I live in them will produce a lot of fruit. But you can't produce

18

He is the vine.

The vine is the trunk of the plant. It's the big part that has all the roots and grows out of the ground.
And the branches are us.
Believers live in him, get our strength and our life from the trunk, the vine, Jesus.

And the vinedresser is God.

He walks the vineyard and tends to the branches, pruning them, cutting them and cleaning them. The vinedressers main goal is to grow more fruit. The more the better.

Jesus says that if you live in him

you will bear lots of fruit.
And if you don't live in him then you aren't going to grown any fruit.

anything without me. Whoever doesn't live in me is thrown away like a branch and dries up. Branches like this are gathered, thrown into a fire, and burned. If you live in me and what I say lives in you, then ask for anything you want, and it will be yours. You give glory to my Father when you produce a lot of fruit and therefore show that you are my disciples."

John 15:1–8

Let's get the picture. It's a beautiful sunny day in the middle of an amazing vineyard. The roots are old and big. They climb up the trellis and shoot out all kinds of branches that are covered with leaves and fruit. The vinedresser is there, tending to his most prized possession, working his hardest to get the most fruit he possibly can out of his plant. He has on his big brimmed hat and his tough work gloves. He has a bucket of water and a sponge. He moves across the vineyard, picking up the weak branches that are crawling along the ground and cleaning the mold off of them; he rubs off the mud and places them on the trellis high up in the sun so that they can start to grow fruit. He cuts off the smaller shoots, refusing to let them crowd out the fruit that will come on the bigger branches. He prunes, he cuts, and he does it all in a gentle, loving way that will nurture and encourage the growth of fruit.

What's going on here is pretty amazing, really, but you wouldn't really get the full extent of just how amazing without fully understanding the job of the vinedresser. His goal is not to stress out the vine or the branches. He's not working out of anger, chopping haphazardly. He's not even cutting just to make things look better. He's working with a purpose, and every move he makes has one goal: to improve the production of the plant.

But what does this pretty scene have to do with you, God, and Jesus?

This scene is the symbol of your life. It's like this: when you are down in the dumps, in the dark mud, growing all kinds of mold and producing wimpy pieces of fruit, the vinedresser—God—comes along and cleans you, lifts you up, and gets you out into the sun. When God forbids you to do stuff but you do it anyway out of weakness or rebellion or just because you can, your vine gets sick and dirty. And when that happens, fruit can't grow. You're not healthy enough to produce anything good, and so you get moldy and muddy. And life starts to feel out of control.

But the vinedresser is there working, cleaning, doing his part to increase your fruit. If you look at that

21

list of fruit and see any of it lacking in your life, then your fruit production is lower than it could be, and that's when things start to get shaken up. Things get cut and pruned and moved around. That cutting and pruning hurts. It's not pleasant as it's happening to you. But the result can be amazing if you are willing to let the vinedresser do the work.

A God Girl, by definition, is a girl connected to God. Not a girl who likes God or who is interested in God but one who is connected to him. A God Girl knows that she must remain attached to the vine, continually get strength and nourishment from it, and never move away from it.

All this branch and vine talk can sound weird. You hear people talking about abiding in Christ and staying in him. But what does that mean in your day-to-day life? How do you work that out practically?

God Girl is here to help you figure that out. As you read through this book, I hope you find practical ways to stay connected to Christ when it comes to your friends, your family, boys, your enemies, and even strangers. I also hope you learn what it means when it comes to knowing yourself and how to express yourself to the world around you. So let's take a look at the life of a God Girl and see how becoming more like her will change your life for the better.

2

A Girl Who Knows Love

Dear friends, we must

love each other because love comes from God.

Everyone who loves
has been born from God
and knows God.
The person who doesn't love
doesn't know God,
because God is love.

1 John 4:7–8

When I was a little girl, my biggest hero was my dad. I adored him. Any chance I got to be with him, I would drop everything else, no matter how cool. He always trumped everything and everyone. In my eyes he could do no wrong; he was pure perfection.

Then, when I was twelve, my world crashed in around me when he left us. He and my mom were fighting one night, and then he was gone. I was young, I didn't understand, and I was hurt, broken, and sorely bruised. I hated him. And my heart hardened. I spent the next few years resenting him and doing everything I could to distance myself from him. To this day I still have moments of regret—moments of deep longing where I wish that I could go back and just be his kid again. Go to the grange co-op with him and buy feed. Get on the tractor and buck hay in the hot sun. Things I got to do for such a short time, I want back.

Inside every girl is a longing to have the perfect love relationship with her father. No matter how great or how horrible he actually was as father, we all deeply desire more intimacy with the first man in our lives. Your dad, just like mine, will forever be a part of your heart, no matter what he's done or not done. A girl's father is her first love, her evidence that there truly is a God and that he truly loves her. I believe each of our hearts carries a blueprint that points directly to a pure, untainted love from a father that will never disappoint. Your earthly father can never be all the love that you need. He is simply your shot at a quick look at the original Father. And no matter what your father was like or is like,

25

God's love is here to stay, and that's what gives the God Girl the strength to rise above the mess and to smile.

no matter how he loved or hated, no matter who your father here on earth is, your Father in heaven is truly in love with you. He's the reality that a father on earth should be a reflection of.

If your dad wasn't a good reflection of God the Father, I am so sorry. I know how you feel, and I'm sorry. But we must remember that our dads are only human and the love we long for does exist—and it is more abundant than anything here on earth. You see, God is not only the author of love, he is love (see 1 John 4:8). When I first met God face-to-face, I was most shaken by the fact that he, unlike my earthly father, was there for good. I couldn't believe that the father figure I had dreamt of and yearned for was right there all along. And no matter what I did or how badly I messed up, he wasn't walking out, period. He even wrote it down, like a contract, a guarantee of his faithfulness, right there for all of us to read in the amazing book of Romans:

I am convinced that nothing can ever separate us from God's love which Christ Jesus our Lord shows us. We can't be separated by death or life, by angels or rulers, by anything in the present or anything in the future, by

26

forces or powers in the world above or in the world below, or by anything else in creation.

Romans 8:38–39

God's love is here to stay, and that's what gives the God Girl the strength to rise above the mess and to smile. She knows that no matter how hard life may be, no matter how bad she's messed up, he will never abandon her and never leave her (see Hebrews 13:5). And that's what makes loving him back such a sure thing. When you can know beyond a shadow of a doubt that he is faithful and never walks out, you can feel free to love him with all your heart, with all your soul, with all your mind, and with all your strength (see Mark 12:30).

Love is the best way to describe God.

He is, by definition, love; therefore, everything that he does is out of love. Everything that he says, thinks, feels—it is all formed in love. So that means that love is the most important thing in the life of a girl whose goal is to be the example of God's love to the world. Everything else that you will ever do rests on your understanding of His love. There is no commandment, no rule, no requirement that isn't built on love. And that's good news. Love is not only the most amazing thing in the world; it is also the foundation of faith. Jesus put it like this:

"Love the Lord your God with all your heart, with all your soul, and with all your mind." This is the greatest and most important commandment. The second is like it: "Love your neighbor as you love yourself." All of Moses' Teachings and the Prophets depend on these two commandments.

Matthew 22:37–40

Love is the highest goal of the God Girl (see 1 Corinthians 14:1). It's her gift to the Creator. It's her expression of thanks, praise, and honor. It defines her: "Everyone will know that you are my disciples because of your love for each other" (John 13:35). When she loves she obeys the two greatest commandments and so fulfills the rest of them. Love is the doorway into a life of faith, and it gives back to the God Girl as much as she gives it away. Love never disappoints. We may face earthly rejection or pain, but when a girl obeys God's call to love, she is rewarded in ways that are often unseen.

The underlying truth about love, however, is that it makes life easier. When you learn to love no matter what the circumstances, you learn to rise above. You gain hope and confidence, and your life is made better by the simple fact that you choose love over anger, hate, frustration, or bitterness. Love is the fuel of a healthy and holy life.

What Does Love Look Like?

But what is love? It is such a massive concept that it can be hard to really know how to do it. So let's take a look at some of the basics of loving others God's way in everyday life.

The God Girl with Her Friends

The God Girl loves her friends effortlessly. She seems to be so kind and loving that no one can hold anything against her. She is easy to be around. She isn't demanding or selfish; she lives outside of herself. She truly cares about what her friend has to say and listens well. She gives up the best seat in the theater so her friend can have it. She doesn't fight with her over boys or clothes. She isn't easily hurt or angered (see 1 Corinthians 13:5) because love doesn't mean getting what you want when you want it but means giving what others need. When the world sees the God Girl, she looks different than most girls because she is selfless (see Matthew 16:24). She considers others more important than herself (see Philippians 2:3–4), and that makes her love unique. In all her

"If you are hard and vindictive,
insistent on your own way,
certain that the other person is
more likely to be in the wrong than you are,
it is an indication that there are
whole tracts of your nature
that have never been transformed
by His gaze."

—Oswald Chambers

relationships there is a taste of Jesus. People want to be around her because she makes them feel important and loved. Friendship, to her, is about not what she can get but how she can draw others to Jesus and be his hands and feet. The God Girl is the best friend another girl can have.

But what happens when things get tough and friendship gets messy? How does the God Girl deal with a critical friend or a jealous friend? What if her friend is changing, drifting away? How does the God Girl deal with adversity in friendship?

With confidence. The God Girl has **confidence** in her God and in his **sovereignty**, and therefore she never panics. She doesn't retaliate when friends get nasty. She doesn't have to fight; she has to **love**. She doesn't demand loyalty of anyone but herself. And so when things get tough, she remains **calm, kind, and hopeful.** She gives others what they want, not what she wants. **Love always puts others first**; it's never irritable or vengeful, because it lives for a greater purpose. To **love** is to be the breath of Christ to the world. So when the **God Girl loves**, she always puts **Christ first**, not her wants or needs. The God Girl is the best friend the world can have.

You might not feel like the most loving friend. You may have messed up in the past, but you can't let that determine your future. Love takes practice. You're going to make mistakes, but that's okay. You can't let failure become a reason to give up; make it a reason to try all the harder. When you love the way God designed you to love, not only will you find more love for yourself, but your life will have less drama and destruction in it. People will be drawn to you, and even if they aren't, you will be okay with that.

So don't let the job ahead of you scare you. Just trust that love is yours to give and that you can be the most amazing friend by the power of the living God.

The God Girl with Her Family

Sometimes the hardest people to love can be the ones who are closest to you. I know that I don't get as frustrated with my friends as I do with my mother. And I bet the same is true for you. But the God Girl has to make an amazing effort to bring peace to the home.

In Jesus's parable of the vine and the branches (see John 15:1–8), he tells us how each one of us who belongs to him are part of the vine. Can you imagine the branch of a plant lashing out and trying to hurt the branch right next to it? It would be like hurting itself. And that's what we do when we fight with our families. We are a part of one another, and we must love each other.

In fact, you've probably heard it a million times, but let's make it a million and one: you must "Honor your father and your mother, so that you may live for a long time in the land the LORD your God is giving you" (Exodus

20:12). **Honoring them means that you don't argue with them in anger or bitterness.** You don't roll your eyes or ignore them, but you give them the respect God commands you to give them. You might discuss differences and disagreements with them, but you always respect them as the authority over you, like a boss or a teacher. As a **God Girl** you are the fragrance of God even to your family. Each person you live with has their own story, their own walk. And each one has their own problems. As a God Girl, your gift of loving them is a gift of refreshing.

Home should be not a war zone but a refuge. When you love your family, you help it to be that for them, but also for you. The God Girl loves her family, no matter how crazy or how bad they are, because she knows that God purposed her for this exact family and that her role in it is crucial. She can either be a change agent in their lives and her own, or she can resign herself to misery and despair. The God Girl always chooses hope, faith, and love. And those choices demand a love that never gives up and always believes. Love your family and you will find love for yourself.

But how does loving your family look? You've probably heard this all before, but have still had your share of family drama.

So how about some help. Here are some things to think about when it comes to your family.

1. Ask yourself what God wants to teach you through this person or problem. Be real: if the same problems happen over and over again, what leads up to them? Trace your steps. Then see if God doesn't want you to change something. Your life will never advance and you will never grow if you aren't willing to look at your problems and take some of the blame—or at least take some action towards making them better.

2. Apologize. An apology covers up a lot of problems. When you fight with your family, apologize. You can surely find something you did wrong. It will help soften the situation.

3. Don't escalate the conflict. Think about your relationship with God. How does he want you to react? This doesn't depend on how others are acting but on what would please God.

4. Be willing to be wronged. Jesus never fought back when people accused him of things. He didn't argue. So why do you have to? Be willing to be wrong in someone's eyes, knowing that God knows your heart.

If you want more help on loving your family, you'll find more in my book *Stupid Parents* than I could ever write here.

The God Girl with Boys

Take a look at how a God Girl acts with boys. She isn't competitive, always trying to one-up them. She isn't one of the guys. She appreciates them for their differences and doesn't try to make them into her best friend. She knows that a relationship with a boy is a very different thing from one with a girl. She is aware of how boys think and does what she can to protect their hearts and their minds by not leading them on or tempting them. She also knows that their way of relating and hers are very different, so when she is interested in a boy, she doesn't treat him as she wants to be treated but as he would be treated. That means that loving a boy means being willing to hold back a little instead of telling him all of the details of your life. It means allowing there to be some mystery, some unknowns between you.

A God Girl doesn't need a boy to be fulfilled and doesn't need to be heard by him to feel complete. She doesn't ever allow the pursuit of boys to be more important than the pursuit of God, and that makes her very attractive. The confidence that the God Girl has in her relationship with God allows her to not be needy or clingy. **She doesn't chase boys**, call them regularly, or text them many times a day. **She has her own life and is pursuing her own purpose,** and she won't allow her emotions to overshadow that. Therefore, she doesn't let **boys become her obsession** by dreaming of them all day and talking to them all night. Though she feels feelings of excitement and anticipation in his presence she tempers that with other pursuits, choosing to keep her focus on the bigger picture. When a boy is interested in her, she considers herself a prize that he must win and not a phrase waiting to be completed.

You may disagree about your role with boys. You may say this is all too old-fashioned and things have changed. And you would be right. Things have changed. Girls can chase boys. They can be just one of the guys, and they can make a boy their everything. But when they do, they lose the charm and the mystery that God wants them to have. Girls who make the pursuit of a boy their main goal in life look needy and insecure. They don't instill confidence in boys or make them want to fight for her. They make boys lazy and complacent, and they devalue themselves.

A girl with a boy is a magical thing, and when God orchestrates it, nothing is more amazing. But when you attempt to take that job away from God and do it yourself,

Love

is an action,
not a feeling.

How can you be sure that love isn't a feeling? Simple. God commands you to love. And since feelings can't be commanded, love can't be a feeling. See, I can't order you to be giddy right now, it's not possible to turn on those kinds of feelings. But actions can be commanded. I can command you to stand on one foot, and you could easily do it. At least I hope. So, if God is commanding you to love, he isn't talking about how you feel about someone but what you do for them. Love is an action, not a feeling.

you set yourself up for disaster. The most valuable jewel in the world isn't one that you can get at any Wal-Mart or Target; it is the one that is hard to find and comes at a great cost. You are that jewel, and your value ought to be so great that boys have to work for years to gain your affection. The harder he has to work to get you, the more he will value you. Become the rare jewel you were meant to be, and don't give yourself away like just another piece of junk jewelry.

So when it comes to love and boys, the God Girl lives like this:

1. She doesn't ever choose the love of a boy over the love of God (see Galatians 1:10).
2. She guards her heart and doesn't give boys easy access to her deepest thoughts and feelings (see Proverbs 4:23).
3. She isn't jealous (see 1 Corinthians 13:4).
4. She doesn't depend on a boy to be her source of happiness but depends on God (see Galatians 5:22).
5. She never idolizes a guy (see Exodus 20:4).
6. She never fights over a boy (see Matthew 5:44).

The God Girl with Her Enemies

Love by its very nature isn't picky. It doesn't just offer itself to the lovable, but it must be offered to the unlovable as well. If you only love those who love you back, then what good is love to a world that is dying? Jesus asks, "If you love those who love you, do you deserve a reward? Even the tax collectors do that! Are you doing anything remarkable if you welcome only your friends? Everyone does that!" (Matthew 5:46–47). Love must not exclude people who don't love you back. But it must include even your enemies. Jesus makes that clear when he says, "But I tell you this: Love your enemies, and pray for those who persecute you" (Matthew 5:44).

Can you do it? Can you love someone who is out to get you? Someone who wants to hurt you? If not, Jesus asks, then what good is your love? The God Girl doesn't love others because of who they are or what they do but because of who God is and what he has done.

When I was in high school I was the victim of choice for Mean Girls. I know what it's like to have enemies. I know what it's like to be hated. And I can tell you that to hate them back is to lose. But to love them back is to win. God's promise is that he will bless you if you love mean people. And his blessing is far greater than anything you could make for yourself by retaliating. That's why he says, "Don't repay evil for evil. Don't retaliate with insults when people insult you. Instead, pay them back with

39

Selfless Love?

Lately, my Father has revealed to me a depth selfishness in myself that I never even so much as suspected. I find that all my kindness to others, my benevolence, and what seemed to be the most unselfish acts of my life, all have had their root in a deep and subtle form of self-love. My motto has for a long time been "Freely ye have received, freely give" and I dreamed that in a certain sense I was living up to it, not only as regards physical blessings, but spiritual as well.

But I find now that I have never really given one thing freely in my life. I have always expected and demanded pay of some kind for every gift, and where the pay has failed to come, the gifts have invariably ceased to flow. If I gave love, I demanded love in return; if I gave kindness I demanded gratitude as payment; if I gave counsel, I demanded obedience to it, or if not that, at least an increase of respect for my judgment on the part of the one counselled; if I gave the gospel I demanded conversions or a reputation of zeal and holiness; if I gave consideration, I demanded consideration in return. In short I sold everything, and gave nothing. I know nothing of the meaning of Christ's words "Freely ye have received, freely give." But I did it ignorantly.

Now however the Lord has opened my eyes to see something of the nature and extent of this selfishness, and I believe He is also giving me grace to overcome it in a measure. I have been taking home to myself the lesson contained in Matthew 5:39–48. I desire to do everything now as to the Lord alone, and to receive my pay only from Him. His grace must carry on this work in me for I am utterly powerless to do one thing toward it; but I feel assured that He will.

And I feel have to thank Him for what He has already done. He has conquered a feeling of repugnance which was growing in me towards someone with whom I am brought into very close contact, and enabled me to give freely, without even wanting any return. Oh how great He is in strength and wisdom!

—*The Christian's Secret of a Holy Life: The Unpublished Personal Writings of Hannah Whitall Smith* a blessing. That is what God has called you to do, and he will bless you for it" (1 Peter 3:9 NLT).

The God Girl defines herself by her God and not the actions of others. Therefore, she is never a victim. She never feels a need to run away from mean people, because she sees their cruelty as an opportunity to prove that God is more important than anything anyone else could throw at her. Mean people were an essential part of her salvation, because hate and anger were what put Christ on the very cross that saved her. Mean isn't a surprise to God, and for the God Girl it's an opportunity for a new life and a chance to prove the power of love.

So when you find yourself with enemies in your life, determine to be like Christ, who "never verbally abused those who verbally abused him. When he suffered, he didn't make any threats but left everything to the one who judges fairly" (1 Peter 2:23). Christ is your example, so don't be surprised when people hate you, but instead trust your life and your love to the God who never disappoints.

The God Girl with Strangers

The beauty of a God Girl is never more evident than when she is with strangers, because it is in those moments that her kindness and concern for people who can do nothing for her can be seen. It's easy to say that a girl is nice to her friends because they love her or to her family because they are, well, a family. And it can even be argued that she is trying to get her enemies to change and to like her when she loves them back. But when she is loving to a stranger, something magical happens. Those who are watching are intrigued, and those whom she loves are encouraged. Loving people we don't know reminds us that we are all part of the same human race. It gives hope to the lost and offers a small glimpse of the love of God.

When a God Girl meets another human being, she sees not a stranger but another valuable soul. That means that she doesn't ignore the people around her as if they are just extras in the movie in which she is the star. She connects with them, even if only with eye contact and a smile. When she gets onto an elevator, she is friendly, even making small talk. When she sits next to someone in a theater, she says hello. When she is waited on by a server, she talks to her as a person, not as a servant. She takes a genuine interest in the souls around her, whether they are beautiful or not. And because of that she is the sweet aroma of God to the souls she encounters.

When a God Girl sees a stranger in need, she doesn't hesitate to help. She stands up for the weak and the ugly. She makes the human race her family and the family of faith her brothers and sisters. If the God Girl doesn't care for the strangers God puts in her path, she runs the risk of missing out on the call on her life—God's call to love her neighbors as herself.

If you want to be a bridge to God for a dying world, then you must open yourself up to show kindness and compassion to strangers. This is not just a good idea but a command: "Don't forget to show hospitality to strangers, for some who have done this have entertained angels without realizing it" (Hebrews 13:2 NLT). Be willing to trust God and to step out, even though you may fear others' response. This life isn't about how they respond but about how you respond to God's call to love. Be brave, God Girl, and you will surely be rewarded!

When my dad left me—when he gave up on us and went to live his own life—I had to make a choice. At first I chose selfishly, and I hid. I rejected him because I believed he had rejected me. But one day I got tired of the hating and decided to try something new. I knew that if I wanted a loving relationship with my dad, the only way to get it was to give it, expecting nothing in return. And so I broke the wall I had built and I reached out to him. He was still that same man he was when he left. He didn't embrace me and ask my forgiveness, as I dreamt he would. In fact, as I sat before him, vulnerable and crying, expressing my feelings, he peered past me at the football game on TV and shouted something in support of his team. Yep, the same old dad, but at the moment that I allowed him to be human and I chose to love him in spite of his inability to love me back, my heart changed, and that was all that mattered. I didn't get my dream dad, but many years later I did get an "I love you." That was something I don't recall hearing in all of my childhood. And it meant the world.

Now he's my dad. We talk and we hug, and we say "I love you" quite regularly. Love is never in vain—even if a person never returns your affection, I can promise you love is never in vain. Love is your expression of faith. And the Father returns love to anyone who is willing to receive it. "Because you love me, I will rescue you. I will protect you because you know my name" (Ps. 91:14).

Because you love me, I will rescue you. I will protect you because you know my name.
Psalm 91:14

Loving isn't just a suggestion; it's is the very command on which all other commands are based. Without love, we as believers have nothing. But take heart: love never fails. It might be rejected, it might give you pain, but that doesn't make it less valuable or rewarding to your soul. The God Girl will be known by her love. And the love that she offers will impact not only the hearts of those who receive it but the heart of the girl who gives it.

God Girl Checklist

Here are a few practical ways to express what you've learned in this chapter. You don't have to do all of them, but you can. Just look at the list and see which things you think might help you know love.

Turning the other cheek—This week do a study on humility. What is it? How did Jesus exemplify it? Find all the verses on it. Then apply them to your life. Learn how to be humble and to turn the other cheek no matter how crazy it seems. Either God's Word is true all the time, or it's just plain wrong. If you believe it's right, then you've got to act on it no matter what the circumstance.

Love orphans and widows— *"Pure, unstained religion, according to God our Father, is to take care* of orphans and widows when they suffer and to remain uncorrupted by this world" (James 1:27). This week try to find a way to obey God's command to love. Volunteer at a retirement home or boys' or girls' club. Find a way to help those in need, like by getting donations or creating a clothes or food closet at your church for people in need. Take action, and show the world that God changes lives.

Turning hate to love—If you are having a problem obeying God's command to love a mean person in your life, then read or reread *Mean Girls: Facing Your Beauty Turned Beast*. No matter if the mean's coming from a girl or a guy, you have to learn how to apply God's law to every aspect of your life.

Your love list—Feeling blue, unloved, or sad because of your unmet longings? If you are depressed or even blue, then make a list of everything you are thankful for. Write down the names of everyone you love and everything that shows you how much God loves you. Then find a way each day to show your appreciation for one person or thing in your life. For example, spend the day with your mom and talk about her, not you. Or to show you appreciate the roof over your head, clean up the house. Show your appreciation of God's expression of love to you by taking care of it.

God's love list—As a God Girl you have to know what pleases God so you can know what to do. So find out what pleases him. Then write it down. Get a blank journal that will be your "God Loves" list. Then make a list of things that God loves. He loves obedience, humility, kindness, peace, and so on. Write down all the verses you can find that apply to each thing that he loves. Over time, if you keep this up, you'll have a nice little book filled with all the things that make the God you love happy. Well, *the book* won't make God happy but *you living it out* will make him rejoice. And every time you make God happy, you are sure to find peace and love for yourself.

3

A Girl Who Knows True Happiness

When I was eighteen I had ulcers.

The cause? My thoughts. I inflicted pain on my body by thinking sinful thoughts. I was obsessed with worry. I felt like the weight of the world was on me and the only way I could hold it up was to continually think about it and fear the worst. I made worry a daily part of my life, peppered with an unhealthy dose of doubt, and I was a wreck. When I was in my early twenties I considered suicide. My life, according to my way of thinking, was so out of control that the only way out of it was to end it. Luckily I had good friends who wouldn't let that happen and stayed with me until I got my mind back where it needed to be. Imagine if I had grabbed the knife at that moment—I wouldn't be talking to you now. Wow, how a life can change.

I was a believer when those thoughts tried to control me. But I had yet to truly take God's Word and call it mine, and instead I served the god of my feelings. If I felt it, it must be true. That was my nature. But as I dug deeper into God's Word, I started to find out the opposite was true. I had often heard and even believed that worry was calling God a liar. After all, he said he is in control and that he will never leave us or forsake us. He said worry is sin. He said to trust him. I knew all that, but it wasn't until I learned the secret to true happiness that I took the step from knowing to doing.

Does your happiness come and go? Do you ever doubt yourself, your God, your faith? Do you have moments of joy followed by moments of despair? Are you tired of the roller coaster? True happiness isn't just for perfect people; us flawed people can have it to. And that's because happiness is based not on circumstances or success but on the very nature of God. He promises to be your joy. You are told to rejoice, or to be happy with him as all you need (see Philippians 4:4). Happiness is found not in your circumstance but in your thoughts.

A girl who knows true happiness is a girl who knows truth and loves it. Unhappiness comes when you know the truth but you aren't so happy about it and when

If you feel like you can't find God,
there is something he wants you to do
that you aren't doing.
Do it, and you'll find him.

you do things that disagree with what you know to be right. When you deep down believe God wants the best for you but you just can't seem to muster the strength to do what you know you should, that's when life gets rocky. A God Girl knows true happiness because she isn't lying to herself about what her heart knows, but she puts all her faith on the fact that God is trustworthy. And because of that, she's going to let 'er rip and put all her hope in him. True happiness is within the reach of anyone willing to risk taking God at his word and refusing to believe anything else, even if she feels it deeply or hears it repeatedly.

I don't believe that true happiness was meant to be an occasional thing or that life was meant to be a roller coaster of emotion. But sometimes that's the case. **Happy comes and happy goes.** But true happiness is something different. It's an undying faith that no matter what happens, "it is well with my soul." It's a steady belief that God is not only all-knowing but also all-powerful, and because of that all of life has meaning, even the bad parts. True happiness isn't turning your back on the harsh realities of life. It isn't grinning in the face of heartache and loss. But it is a steady belief in the God who can and, because of that, a firm belief that "I can! No matter what the odds, I can!" The God Girl may be in mourning, she may be in pain, but she never comes out from under the shelter of the wings of God. She knows that "He will cover you with his feathers, and under his wings you will find refuge. His truth is your shield and armor" (Psalm 91:4).

When your life is lacking true happiness, you can do something.

Life doesn't have to stay the way it is. Happiness can return if you are willing to take God at his word. So let's find out how you can bring true happiness to your life to stay.

Tell Yourself the Truth

The pursuit of truth is the passion of every God Girl. Knowing the truth, loving the truth, and determining to only think things that are true leads her to true happiness. That means that she doesn't allow lies to become part of her vocabulary. "I can't." "I'm scared." "I'm too weak." "Life is too hard." These lies, these things that disagree with God, aren't good for life and hope. They give you the opposite of happiness. They breed despair and fear.

God offers you more. He offers you the most that you could ever receive, and all you have to do is to tell yourself the truth. And the only way to know what that truth is, is to look into the Word of God. In every area where she has trouble, the God Girl searches out the truth and then repeats it to herself. She takes those lies she's been believing and edits them out of her vocabulary. If you want to find true happiness, then take a look at the lies you believe. Here are just a few—do any of them sound familiar?

Some lies we believe:

God could never forgive me.

My life would be better if _____ loved me.

God won't save me from what I fear the most.

The more I worry, the better the chances I can fix things.

I can't handle it when people don't like me.

Anytime you say "I can't," "It's too hard," "I'm depressed," or "I'm afraid"; anytime you panic or worry; anytime you act in anger, bitterness, or frustration— you are lying to yourself. You are saying something that flat out isn't true. I know that because these thoughts and the ones that lead to these conclusions disagree with what God says in his Word.

God's Word is all true, so if what you say or believe is the opposite of God's Word, it's a lie. Lies make you unhappy. They destroy lives and make things difficult. But the truth gives you strength,

God's Word is all true, so if what you say or believe is the opposite of God's Word, it's a lie.

Memories
from the Past

"In my own case I just determined I would be satisfied with God alone. I gave up seeking after any feeling of satisfaction, and consented to go through all the rest of my life with no feeling whatever, if this should be God's will. I said, 'Lord, you are enough for me, just yourself, without any of your gifts or your blessings. I have you, and I am content. I will be content, I choose to be content, I am content.' I said this by faith. I still have to say it by faith often. I have to do so this very evening, for I am not very well, and feel, what I expect thou would call 'low.' But it makes no difference how I feel. He is just the same, and he is with me, and I am His, and I am satisfied."

— Hannah Whitall Smith

hope, and power. So take a look at the truth and see how much the lies get it wrong:

"I can't." "It's too hard." When these words have to do with obeying God's Word they are not true. God never commands you to do something impossible. In fact everything that he commands he will help you to do. That means it's all possible! All of it. "I can't" is a lie—if it's something God wants you to do then your only response is "I must."

"I'm depressed." A depressed mind is a mind focused on lies instead of truth. God's Word, the truth, was given in order to set you free. And knowing his Word and believing it will set you free from your occasional depression. God promises to give joy to those who love him; it is a fruit of the spirit given to those who remain connected to the vine (Galatians 5:22; Ecclesiastes 2:26). And it is a command: *"Always be joyful"* (1 Thessalonians 5:16). Since God never commands the impossible it must be so.

"I'm afraid." In the book of Jeremiah it says, " 'Don't be afraid of people. I am with you, and I will rescue you,' declares the Lord" (Jeremiah 1:8). And in Psalms we read, "So we will not fear when earthquakes come and the mountains crumble into the sea" (Psalm 46:2). When you have fear in your life, go to God's Word and find hope and protection. You are protected by the Creator of the universe. What could harm you? Nothing, except that he allows it for your benefit.

Like Joseph being thrown into jail you must know that God has everything under control and will work all things together for the good of those who love him (Romans 8:28).

All people have sinned, they have fallen short of God's glory. They receive God's approval freely by an act of his kindness through the price Christ Jesus paid to set us free [from sin]. God showed that Christ is the throne of mercy where God's approval is given through faith in Christ's blood.

Romans 3:23–25

I can do everything through Christ who strengthens me.

Philippians 4:13

He will put his angels in charge of you to protect you in all your ways.

Psalm 91:11

Never worry about anything. But in every situation let God know what you need in prayers and requests while giving thanks.

Philippians 4:6

Blessed are you when people insult you, persecute you, lie, and say all kinds of evil things about you because of me.

Matthew 5:11

Take Every Thought Captive

Finally, brothers and sisters, keep your thoughts on whatever is right or deserves praise: things that are true, honorable, fair, pure, acceptable, or commendable.

Philippians 4:8

Happiness is always just a thought away. Think sad thoughts and you'll be sad; think happy thoughts and you'll be happy. That's why God calls you to think about the good things in life, not the bad stuff. Did you know that it isn't what happens to you that makes you miserable but what you *think* about what happens to you that controls your emotions? Your happiness rests in your hands, God Girl. When you refuse to concentrate on the negative parts of life, you take those negative thoughts captive (see 2 Corinthians 10:5). Then all that is left is to replace those thoughts with things that are true, good, praiseworthy, and honorable.

Think about it like this: you get whatever you sow. When you plant a tomato seed in the ground, you don't expect to get a crop of cucumbers. The same is true of your mind: when you fill it with seeds of negative thinking, complaining, and whining, you get negative feelings, depression, anger, and bitterness. But when you plant seeds of hope and faith, you get good feelings—feelings of hope, faith, life, and happiness. Your garden is yours to till and to sow. What kind of crops do you want to harvest? Choose, and then get to work with the seeds of that crop.

So how do you take thoughts captive? It takes two things. The first is that you have to know the law. A police officer can't be good at their job if they don't know the law. They can't arrest people unless they know what's illegal. The same goes for your thoughts. You've got to know what is acceptable and what isn't. So learn God's Word. Find out what he wants from you, and when your mind wanders off into unlawful subjects, grab those thoughts, throw them out the door, and slam it shut. Then turn around and think about something that is lawful. Replace those wrong thoughts with truth. You have to stop the bad thoughts as soon as you notice them, and each time you do, you'll notice them earlier and earlier. You can't let them become a habit. Refuse them each time they pop up, and you'll start to gain more and more control of your own mind.

The God Girl tells herself the truth even though everything inside her argues against it. Learn the truth. Make it your weapon against failure and self-destruction. Don't ever let how you feel dictate what you believe. Feelings lie, but God's Word never does.

Agree with God

The quickest way to happiness is to agree with God, because when you disagree with him, finding

You Are What You Think

"Man is chained only by himself. Thoughts are the jailers of Fate—they imprison, being base; they are also the angels of Freedom—they liberate, being noble. Not what he wished and prays for does a man get, but what he harbors within. His wishes and prayers are only gratified and answered when they harmonize with his thoughts."

—James Allen

the strength to do right is difficult. "No one can please God without faith" (Hebrews 11:6). Can you agree that all of God's Word is good and the best choice for your life? If you cannot, then you are destined to lose out on true happiness. Disagreeing with God's commands can bring instant satisfaction, but over time the result of disagreeing with him and his call on your life will be emotional and spiritual and maybe even physical distress.

Wanna test your thoughts? Think about it like this: any thought that disagrees with God is a lie, because God speaks only truth.

"He is a **rock**.

What he does is **perfect**.

All his ways are **fair**.

He is a faithful **God**,

who does **no wrong**.

He is **honorable**

and **reliable**" (Deuteronomy 32:4).

When you lie to yourself, you sin. And sin leads you away from true happiness. Worry calls God a liar and leads to emotional and physical trauma like ulcers, panic attacks, isolation, and the list goes on. Fear rejects God's truth and leads to depression, paranoia, failure, and much more. Stress says God won't do what God says he will do. But you can't know that if you don't know God's Word. So in order to agree with him, you have to hear him out. You want more peace, more hope? Then you've gotta get into God's Word and find out what he's thinking.

Every time you disagree with God and his Word, you hurt yourself and your relationship with God. If you want true happiness, the kind that never leaves, then you must agree with God on every point and refuse to be moved. And God will give you the happiness that you crave (see Ecclesiastes 2:26).

Get Over It

> Though your sins are bright red, they will become as white as snow. Though they are dark red, they will become as white as wool.
>
> Isaiah 1:18

The God Girl is a girl who doesn't hold on to failure or mess-ups. She believes the Bible when it says that "God is faithful and reliable. If we confess our sins, he forgives them and cleanses us from everything we've done wrong" (1 John 1:9). Therefore, the God Girl doesn't hold on to the past, holding herself hostage to her mistakes. Instead she accepts forgiveness as freely as God gives it, and so refuses to rehash her sin, to punish herself, or to define herself by it. Forgiveness

Disagreement

Here are some ways that you disagree with God.
You disagree with him when you

- doubt
- fear
- worry
- hate
- fight back
- lust
- lose control
- get impatient
- hold a grudge
- get revenge
- resent
- are mean
- get depressed
- hurt yourself
- hurt others
- obsess over something
- over indulge
- refuse to help

is freedom for the God Girl. It gives her a clean slate. It cleanses her and makes her white as snow.

To refuse forgiveness is to argue with God. If you've done something wrong, you can't hang on to it as if you are a particularly hard case, someone too bad for God to forgive. Remember, if Christ's death on the cross isn't enough to forgive your sins, then Christ died for nothing (see Galatians 2:21). Your sin is never a shock to God, and you are never so bad that he won't take you back.

You have to get over the bad things of the past, your sin, and even the sins of others. To hold on to these things is only to torture yourself. When you refuse to get over things, you hold on to sin as if it is your salvation, your only hope, but that is a lie. **Letting go is your hope and your power.** So refuse to hold on to anything—any memory, any worry, or any fear—that is associated with sin.

That means if you are holding a grudge, you've got to let go of it. Holding on to it is a sin. It's not taking a position of power; it's sin, and so it's weakness. So right now, this minute, get over it! If you think getting even with someone is your job, then you've lost your way. Who do you think you are—God? " 'Vengeance is Mine, I will repay,' says the Lord" (Heb 10:30 NKJV). Don't get even. Don't sit around plotting and planning. Get over it. If there is something you can't get over, then you've got a big weakness that is going to tear you down eventually.

Trash Your Idols

An idol is anything that you are obsessed with and can't get out of your mind. Idols aren't just little wooden figurines or golden cows; they are preoccupations of the mind, things you believe will make you happy or relieve your pain or fear. An idol tries to take the place of God by offering you some kind of hope.

I used to have an idol—well, a few, actually, but the worst was shopping. Whenever I got bummed or just worn out, I would go shopping and it would lift my spirits. It would give me relief. But then it wanted more and more of me (or should I say of my money). Shopping became my idol at the point when I couldn't control it anymore.

Idols will run your life and steal your happiness. At first they offer great things, but then they start to control you, to talk to you, to promise you things they can never truly give. If you have anything in your life that you are obsessed with, then you have idol trouble. Is there anything that if I asked you right now to give up, you couldn't? If so, then you have an idol.

Idols are bad for you. They offer a false happiness and have to be trashed in order to get to true happiness. If you want freedom from the things that seem to control you, then you are in luck. All you need to do is to call them what they are, false gods, and then refuse to worship them. That means get them out of your life. Take away their altars. If it's a movie star that obsesses you, take his posters down and stop daydreaming about him. If it's food, refuse to let the call of it control you, but choose to control it by being obedient to God's Word and taking care of your body by eating healthily. Not too much, not too little.

Whatever you do that you hate, that you want to stop but can't seem to, is an idol. Know that God hates it too, and because of that he is by your side to help you kick it out. And remember, he is more powerful than any other god you could find. But he won't ever do it by himself—he wants you to agree with him and to call your idol an idol. You have the power to be idol free; you just have to own it and then use it. When you do, you will find an abundance of true happiness.

Live a Life of Contentment

The God Girl finds true happiness by living a life of contentment. She is content with what she has and even with what she doesn't

God in Mind

You are the branch and he is the vine, so when water, sunlight, and nutrients cover the soil they are drawn up through the vine and into the branches. When you give God the glory, when you do things for him there is a weird occurrence that feeds you as well. Doing things with God in mind, and for his good will always give you the most strength and nourishment. If it is through the vine that you are fed then why wouldn't you give everything you had to the vine?

have. When you tell yourself that you ought to have something you don't have or that what you have is bad, you are discontent. It isn't easy to be content; it takes work, and at times it can feel like you are lying to yourself. After all, how can you say you are content when what you have isn't enough or isn't what you dreamt of? It's a hard question and one that most people would ask.

Finding happy can't depend on things, because when it does those things disappoint or disappear. Sure, happiness can come from stuff. I know that a cute pair of shoes can bring me joy for days. But they eventually lose their new factor, and my happiness meter drops. When you put your hope for happiness anyplace but in the hands of God, you not only are out for failure, but you make bad and even hurtful decisions.

Look at the effects of divorce on kids across the world. When a person decides that a marriage is responsible for their happiness or lack thereof and so walks away when things get tough, they can bring pain to more than just themselves. To this I can attest. I've seen the search for happiness in the eyes of another destroy my family and my heart. And I confess I've done the same thing. I've hurt many a heart over my belief that a particular guy would bring me joy. The mind of a God Girl isn't set on finding happiness only in the world; she holds a firm belief that an unmoving true happiness can be found not here on earth but in the eyes of her Father. When you are willing to put pleasing him above everything else—even above pleasing yourself—you will find the secret to true happiness.

Contentment isn't based on what you have but on who you know. The apostle Paul says that he learned the secret of contentment, whether he had stuff or had nothing, and the secret was that he could do everything through the one who gave him strength (see Philippians 4:13). That one is Christ Jesus. That means that contentment says, "I don't need this or that to do what needs to be done." And it definitely doesn't need anything other than Christ himself to be happy. When Christ becomes all you need, you will find happy all around you, because he never disappoints.

Here are some ways you can practice contentment:

1. Prioritize. Determine that your greatest goal is storing up treasure in heaven, not here on earth (see Matthew 6:20–21). Look at your priorities and connect them to your treasures. Where is what you gain or give with each priority storing up your treasures? If you don't like where your storehouse is located, do something about reprioritizing.

When Christ becomes all you need, you will find happy all around you, because he never disappoints.

2. Simplify. Find contentment and happiness in learning to live with less (see Matthew 8:20; Acts 4:32).

3. Help others. Knowing that contentment for the God Girl comes from pleasing God, find contentment by getting outside yourself and helping those in need (see Proverbs 21:13; 1 John 3:17).

4. Learn to enjoy what you do have. Use it, love it, share it (see 1 Timothy 6:8).

Find Happiness on the Other Side of Heartache

As a God Girl you don't have to be happy all the time. You are a real human being, with real feelings and real circumstances that will lead to grief and mourning, excitement and joy. And none of that is wrong. In fact, the apostle Paul tells us to "Be happy with those who are happy. Be sad with those who are sad" (Romans 12:15). There is room in the life of a God Girl to feel more than just happiness. But happiness is always the preferred emotion, is it not? And when things get painful and hard to handle, happiness is always that thing that you wish you could find.

I remember when I broke off my first engagement. I was deeply in love with him. I hadn't met anyone like him, and I was sure I wanted to marry him. But there came a point during our engagement when I started to see big red flags waving in my direction. He was panicked, scared even, to marry me. He was starting to become mean and easily angered. His treatment of me went from loving to bitter. And I knew what had to be done, so I let him go. I set him free. I can remember telling him that we needed to call things off. It hurt so bad when he didn't object, but to his credit he didn't. Smart guy. He knew it wasn't going to work, and I'm sure he was thankful that I agreed. And so that moment, we went our separate ways. Period. The end. At least technically it was the end. But emotionally it was only the beginning.

I cried so hard for so long that my friends had to take turns sitting with me on my bed and holding me. That's all they could do. I was inconsolable. I wailed, I mourned, I grieved the loss of the marriage I had dreamt of. It took me a long time to get over him. But each day it got better. And I noticed that it got better the more I looked away from the situation and at the potential. I decided to find the good in the pain. And the good was that the pain drove me to my knees. The pain made me need my God more than I ever had, and that was good. So I told the pain it was over—I was no longer afraid of being alone, of losing him, but was focusing on how God can use the brokenhearted.

The old Bible that Greg handed me so many years ago has a little phrase written inside that has been my inspiration in times of testing. He gave the credit to A. W. Tozer, but I can't be sure that's who said it. Anyway, it deeply impacted my life, so here it is: "God does not use you greatly until he hurts you deeply." When pain comes at you from outside of yourself (in other words, when it isn't self-inflicted), you can be sure that God wants to use it to make you stronger and more devoted. But he can't do that if you aren't willing to see the strength in it, the power to turn away from introspection and to God's Word and truth. Happiness comes on the wings of pain, when you allow pain to do its work. No one can find happiness in the hard times better than a God Girl, because happiness depends on knowing God's hand is at work no matter what the circumstance (see Romans 8:28).

When people hurt me and I feel alone and lonely and desperately want for someone to say, "I know how you

"I conquered my sadness by letting it become a tool in the hand of God to draw me closer to him and farther from my self-pity."

feel," or "I think you are the most amazing person in the world," but no one is there to say it, I go to my room. I shut the door, I lay down on my bed, and I talk.

I talk and talk with God.

I tell him how I feel and how I hurt, and I cry. I beg him to hear my cries, and then I shut up and listen. I wait for him to come to be God to me—the one who comforts and counsels me (see Isaiah 9:6; 2 Corinthians 1:4). Knowing what I know about him, I can easily trust that he will not leave me in my misery. Instead, he will point out to me where I am seeing the world with human eyes instead of godly eyes. He shows me the most important things, like learning to love others, even the mean ones, and learning to live only on the love of God and no one else.

He is truly all you need, my friend, all you need. If you are broken and hurting, you have one who never disappoints and never leaves you. Find a way to get to him. Cry to him, but also remember to listen. His way of thinking is different from the world's. He will never talk to you about what you deserve and should have but will tell you what you don't need to worry about or fear. **Happiness comes quickly when you turn your eyes away from your needs and back to your God.** When your needs become your focus, you are bound to find sadness, because in this world you will never get everything you want. Jesus confirmed it when he said, "I've told you this so that my peace will be with you. In the world

I've told you this so that my peace will be with you. In the world you'll have trouble. But cheer up! I have overcome the world.

John 16:33

you'll have trouble. But cheer up! I have overcome the world" (John 16:33). You can trust his words. You can trust that he has something greater for you than what you are worried about right now, and if you are just willing to look into his eyes and fall into his arms, he will show it all to you.

Your life is full of possibilities. Even in pain and heartache, your life can flourish. Some of the most amazing souls in the world are souls who underwent great pressure and heartache. People like Corrie ten Boom who not only survived a Nazi concentration camp but thrived in it, leading Bible study and worship each night for her fellow prisoners. Women like Joni Eareckson Tada who, though completely paralyzed, has become a world-renowned artist and author. When you refuse to let circumstances dictate who you are and what you will achieve, instead of drowning in the depths of monotony, isolation, pain, and even disaster you can rise and ride on those waves to reach great heights of success and faith.

True happiness is within your reach. There is no need to ride the roller coaster of emotions that the world takes for granted. The life of the God Girl is one of complete trust in the words of God. She knows that "all things work together for the good of those who love God—those whom he has called according to his plan" (Romans 8:28). And because of that, she is fearless and full of hope. Hope produces true happiness because hope believes anything is possible. Hope doesn't despair; it doesn't doubt; it believes. Trust God with your life and trust his Word, and you will have more happiness than you know what to do with.

> I am convinced that nothing can ever separate us from God's love which Christ Jesus our Lord shows us. We can't be separated by death or life, by angels or rulers, by anything in the present or anything in the future, by forces or powers in the world above or in the world below, or by anything else in creation.
>
> Romans 8:38–39

God Girl Checklist

My obsessions—What are you obsessed with? Think about it. What do you spend most of your time thinking about? Is it affecting your emotions? Your relationships? Your spirit? If you don't like what your thoughts are doing to you, then this week make a change. Note all of your obsessions and make a plan for getting rid of them. Obsessed with your computer? Cut down your time on it to one hour per day. Obsessed with sugar? Get the problem out of the house. Make it hard for you to obsess about anything other than God. Check out my book *Idol Girls: What's Your Obsession?* for more help getting rid of obsessions that steal your happy.

Getting over it—Are there some things in your past you just haven't gotten over? What are they? Try this. This week spend some time in worship. Tell God how great he is. Adore him. Then ask him to point out the things you aren't willing to let go of but need to. As things come to mind, write them down. Then tell God thank you for his forgiveness and tell him you agree with him that what is done is done. Refuse to sin longer by holding on to your sin. Once you have a list of things, or even just one, write a prayer. Confess how you have gone wrong by holding on to your sin. Promise to let go. And express your belief that God is big enough to take the stain of it away. He might not remove the consequences, but you can thank him for them because they taught you what was wrong. Don't allow anything to be used for bad, but let it be used only for good.

Toss your thoughts—When Michael and I were dating, I was still dealing with a lot of stress, fear, and worry. One day he took me to the river and handed me a bag of rocks. On each rock was written one of my sins—worry, fear, and so on. He told me to take each one, say it out loud, repent from it, and then throw it into the water. It was a powerful visual of God's power to remove my sin from me as far as the east is from the west. Throwing my sin into the depths of the water never to be seen again gave me strength and reminded me that I was in control of my thoughts, not the world or the circumstances that surrounded me. So if you are willing, try this experience yourself. No river nearby? Go to a cliff and throw them off. Or write them on paper and burn it in a bucket or push it through a paper shredder. Just create a symbol of getting rid of the things that you think often that call God a liar.

Simplify—Wanna practice not loving things of this world? Then give simplicity a try. Go through your stuff and give away, sell, or trash ten things. If there is something you cannot let go of, ask yourself, "Why? What does it mean to me?" Simplicity helps you keep the main thing the main thing and make "things" unimportant. Do some research on the practice of simplicity and give it a chance.

4

A Girl Who Knows
How to
Communicate

Everything you say or do
should be done in the name of the
Lord Jesus, giving thanks to God
the Father through him.

Colossians 3:17

I don't know about you, but I love talking. Talking is so much fun. When I get to talk to someone I feel like we bond, especially if we really hit it off and can talk effortlessly. Ah, I love that.

Before I knew Jesus I was a nasty talker. I loved cussing. I could use a cuss word in every single sentence. I had a foul mouth. And what I said affected the way people around me saw me and treated me. After I got to know Jesus and his character and love, my communication style changed. I suddenly sounded different; I looked different; I was different. And people saw it.

When I got saved I was dating a boy who wasn't a Christian. And within a few weeks he was gone. Literally. I called him up and I couldn't find him. He didn't answer any of his phones, and none of his friends would tell me where he was. He dumped me. The trouble was that he liked the old me, not the new me. And that was too bad. But over time I healed and life went on. Then a few years later I got a call from this boy. He was crying; he needed help. He had hit rock bottom and he wanted Jesus. He knew nothing of my faith but my transformation, and he wanted what I had. That night I led him to Christ, and he took Jesus's hand and began to walk with him. It was a wonderful feeling. When your life and your way of communicating affects the life of someone who needs Jesus, it is an amazing thing.

The God Girl is oftentimes the only Bible that others will read. That means that as a God Girl, you must be aware that what you say, how you talk, and how you communicate with others can affect the eternity of the people around you. As a God Girl your speech and ways of communicating reflect the character of God. When you are kind, compassionate, and listening, people catch a glimpse of the heavenly, and it can give them hope. You must never underestimate your impact on the world. The God Girl knows the world is watching—and they aren't watching her but Christ in her—so she works hard to communicate the love and grace of the Christ who first loved her.

Being a God Girl means being aware of what your words and actions are saying about your God. So let's look at some ways you can communicate his love.

83

Show Kindness

Kindness is charming. It draws others in and makes them feel welcome. Kindness can soften even the meanest of hearts. When people who are serving me are short with me, angry, or just disinterested, I always show them extra kindness. I try to get into their world, stop their cycle of cynicism, and bring a smile to their day. It isn't much, but it is a taste of the kindness and love of Christ, and it might change their entire day. In fact, in some cases, one act of kindness could save their entire life. You can never underestimate the value of kindness, and for a God Girl, anything less is unacceptable. God's kindness to you is your inspiration and your model for your kindness to the world. Kindness is a simple expression of love that opens up a world of possibilities.

Being a God Girl means being aware of what your words and actions are saying about your God.

Being kind isn't always easy, though. Mean people, grumpy people, busy people don't make it easy. Kindness isn't always the easiest response to those types of people, but it needs to be our response (see Psalm 39:1). When I met one of my Mean Girls a few years after graduation, she actually apologized for how mean

84

they had been to me. I looked at her, smiled, and said, "Oh, that's okay. We were just kids." She looked at me with frustration and said, "Dang, why do you have to be so nice about it? Now I feel even more guilty." Kindness not only draws out the kindness of others but also reminds them of their meanness; it convicts them. Refusing to be kind never achieves good results. It only makes things worse. Sure, it feels good to retaliate or to ignore someone, but the end result isn't good (see Proverbs 15:1).

The God Girl makes every effort to be kind to everyone, no matter who they are or what they can or can't do for her (see Proverbs 17:27). Kindness is her gift to a busy and stressed out world. Here are some practical ways to practice kindness every day:

1. Smile at people. A smile can change a person's day and make them feel connected. When you don't smile, people can assume you are too arrogant or mean, even though you may be just thinking about something else. So do your best to smile at people you meet, walk past, or look at.

2. Look them in the eyes. Looking people in the eyes is kindness. It says to them, "You count." And it reminds them that we are all part of the same human race. When you avoid looking people in the eyes, you seem cold and unattached, and that doesn't help to spread the love of Christ but hides it.

3. Offer a hand. When someone is struggling with something heavy, offer them a hand. When someone looks lost, ask them if you can help. When you offer to help people, you share kindness with them and lighten their load.

4. Say hello. In today's busy world it's easy to become isolated from the others, oblivious to the pain and concern of the people around us. But kindness gets involved; it steps into the lives of others, even if only to say hi. Say hi to anyone who looks you in the eyes. Say hi to people who wait on you or serve you in any way. Even if they don't look at you, interrupt their isolation and say hello.

5. Give. Kindness gives to people in need. I can remember when I saw a woman in front of me in line who couldn't buy everything she had in her cart and was putting something back. I said, "Here, I can cover it." I handed a couple of bucks to the clerk and paid for her stuff. Kindness finds a need and helps where it can.

Put Others First

The beauty of the God Girl is that she **isn't about "me" all the time.** She lives outside of herself. She sees other people and takes notice of their pain, their joy, their fear. She is forever thinking from an eternal perspective and is confident enough in her relationship with Christ to know that life is not about her but about loving others so that they might know him as she does.

That's why in all her speech, **she puts others first.** She doesn't monopolize conversations, insisting others hear all about her feelings and thoughts. But she asks a lot of questions and listens to the answers. She draws people out. She doesn't talk to be heard or to feel better. And she knows that if what she has to say is only to make herself feel good, then it's best if it's not said. **She isn't self-seeking and doesn't need the approval of others to be secure,** so she takes her baggage and her stuff to her God and lets others be free from the burden. That means that talking with her is easy. She doesn't always turn the conversation back to herself, and she responds to what people are saying with more than an "Oh," or "I see." She makes conversation about things that interest the people she is talking to. Talking has become a selfish activity for many, but for the God Girl it is an opportunity to give others the gift of human interaction and support.

When in doubt, listen (see Proverbs 17:27-28). The biggest trap for us girls who love to talk is to talk so much we forget that other people have things to say and want to be heard. Keeping quiet can oftentimes be a gift when your talking is replaced with active listening. So in all your speech, always be thinking of *balance*.

Share yourself, but be willing to get off the subject of you and onto the subject of the one you are with.

If you find it hard to shut off the mouth and open up the ears, think about trying some of these things next time you're going to hang out with someone:

1. Pray for them. Before you meet up with someone, pray for them. Praying for them gets your mind on the big picture and off of yourself.

2. Get some questions. Before you go, think of at least five things you want to ask the person about themselves. Like an interviewer interviewing a famous person, take some time to think about what you could ask them that would start a good conversation about them.

3. Praise them. Try to find at least two things about them to praise. When you are looking for the good in them, you won't be thinking about yourself as much.

Respect Authority

"Anyone who rebels against authority is rebelling against what God has instituted, and they will be punished" (Romans 13:2 NLT). The God Girl understands that anyone who has authority over her must be respected. For a lot of us it's easier to respect friends and acquaintances than it is to respect people in authority over us, and that's probably because they are telling us what to do. But parents, bosses, teachers, police—anyone in authority is to be respected even if they are telling you to do something you hate. Respect, according to Romans 13:2, isn't based on how you feel about the person making demands but on their position of God-given authority in your life.

Because of this, the God Girl is respectful of those in authority. Others are always watching the God Girl to see if she is truly who she says she is, and a lack of respect for authority betrays a sinful heart that only confirms that her faith isn't changing her or making her more holy. Obedience to human beings isn't always easy. They are imperfect, they may say things wrong, and they may get things wrong, but that doesn't excuse disrespect. Your life can't be controlled by others' imperfections but should be ruled by God's perfection. That means you must always act out of love for him, not reaction to them.

When a girl respects authority she stands tall, she is confident, she looks others in the eye, she promptly agrees to do what is asked, and she shows a level of honor and a fear of God that makes her easy to work with and live with. When you respect those in authority, you respect the God who put them there. Don't ever let bad authority figures be an excuse for

your bad behavior, but prove yourself good and true by being obedient and respectful.

In order to respect authority:

1. Don't argue. When you argue with authority, you refuse authority. Bite your tongue and obey God.

2. Don't roll your eyes when you disagree. It's okay to disagree with authority in your mind, but you can't be disrespectful by making your disagreement known, unless you do it in a respectful and godly way.

3. Don't mock them when they aren't around. Others who are around are listening, so don't show them how to dishonor authority by complaining or mocking it.

4. Don't ignore them. When someone in authority asks you to do something or even just talks to you, never ignore them. It is disrespectful and only makes the person who ultimately has control over you angry. Not a good situation.

Listen

I have a friend who loves to talk. She talks and talks and tells me everything about her life. Then when I get a chance to tell her something about my life, she listens, but as soon as I am done with a few sentences, she changes the subject back to her. And it hurts.

Listening is more than being quiet while someone talks. It is a gift of communication that you give to

A girl is a God Girl when...

she stops whining and blaming and starts to look for the hidden justice of God. And as she starts to focus her thoughts on that justice of God, she stops blaming other people for her problems and heartache and builds up her holy nature. She stops fighting her circumstances and instead looks at them as tools in the hand of God to move her closer to him and to give her the strength that is part of being a God Girl.

Listening is more than being quiet while someone talks. It is a gift of communication that you give to people you care about.

people you care about. Listening is actually hearing what the person says and responding to it in a way that makes them feel heard and understood. A God Girl knows that listening is required in order for there to be love and a personal connection. Two people can never truly know each other if one or both refuse to listen. For the longest time this friend of mine didn't even know what I did for a living. Can you imagine talking to someone for months on end without even knowing anything about them? It's not that unusual, but it shouldn't be like that in the life of the God Girl.

When people talk, make the effort to stop thinking about yourself and start thinking about them. Here's how to be a good listener:

1. Try to comment on what they are saying. Don't let them say something without saying at least, "I know what you mean," or, "That's too bad." Let them know you are listening by saying something that confirms it.

2. Focus on them. The worst thing is to talk to someone who is looking around the room, reading a book, or watching TV. Try giving people your undivided attention. Then they will know they are being heard.

Don't Talk Just to Be Heard

I always try to think about this quote I once read from a really, really dead guy named Sulpitius Severus: "Speak only when it would be sinful to be silent." What a concept, huh? The Bible kind of confirms it in Proverbs when it says, "Sin is unavoidable when there is much talk, but whoever seals his lips is wise" (Proverbs 10:19). Talk too much and you get yourself in trouble.

Sometimes it's fun to talk just to be heard. But two problems come out of that way of thinking. One is that you wear people out with your words. Talking can be really selfish when you talk just to be heard. If what you want to say isn't useful to build people up or to communicate your love for them, then you have to consider your motives. If you are talking just to be heard, you are being selfish. Talking isn't a sport or an outlet for your energy; it's a tool used to convey the love of God and the kindness of his kids. Sure, you can have fun and talk with your friends, laugh and play,

but take a break every once in a while and give your mouth a break. Talking too much can lead to self-obsession, not God obsession.

Another problem when you talk to people too much is that you leave nothing to work through with God. It's easy to work everything out in your mind by talking to people, and while that can be good, it is also good to spend some of your working out time with God so that you can focus on something outside yourself, something more noble and godly. I've had many times when I wanted to talk to someone about my sadness, my anger, or my problems and couldn't find anyone to listen. So I would go to my room alone to talk to God, and every time it paid off. It was like God made sure there was no one else I could talk to so I would be forced to talk to him.

It's always a good rule of thumb to never talk just to be heard. The God Girl doesn't feel the need to be heard by anyone but God, so she doesn't take up all the talk time with her own words, and that makes her much better at listening to and caring for others.

"O LORD, set a guard at my mouth. Keep watch over the door of my lips."

Psalm 141:3

Don't Complain

"Do everything without complaining or arguing" (Philippians 2:14). To complain is to say that God isn't good because what he has given you isn't good. Complaint is not only sinful but also ugly to those who watch. It makes them feel uncomfortable. It is exhausting to those who listen and ungrateful to those who provide. When a girl complains, she accuses—she either accuses God of having inadequacies or accuses others of the same.

Most of my life I've had a problem with complaining. I saw it not as bad but as communicating my feelings. I always felt that if I didn't voice my feelings about things, then I wasn't being honest. And honesty was always my policy. So I complained about everything. It wasn't until someone pointed out the ugliness of complaint that I woke up and saw it for what it was: a sin. Now when I feel dissatisfied I keep my mouth shut, and I try to find something good about the situation.

Complaint betrays a sense of pride. It says, "I'm worth more than this. I deserve better." And it is never attractive or desired. The God Girl is keenly aware of the impact even the smallest word can have on her spirit and the spirits of those around her, and because of that she avoids complaining at all costs.

Don't Gossip

Gossip can be the glue that binds friend to friend. It's a way to be in agreement, a way to have things in common, and it can be very fun and exciting. But gossip is destructive (see Psalm 15:1–3; Proverbs 16:28) as well as sinful. The **God Girl** can be *trusted*. She doesn't find enjoyment in hurting others with her words. And because of that, she is **loved**. Gossip separates friends. It builds walls. It betrays a superior attitude that is inconsistent with the life of Christ. Whenever a chance to gossip comes along, the God Girl changes the subject or explains her tendency to gossip and her conscious desire to stop it. She doesn't want to be involved in anything that contradicts God's Word, so she will never be a gossip. If anything you hear or say isn't something that will build up the person you are talking about, then it need not be said. Avoid gossip and give others the gift of trust.

But what do you do when your friends start to gossip and tell you about so-

and-so? Well, there are a couple of things you can do. Give these a try:

1. When girls start to gossip around you, excuse yourself. Say that you are working on getting rid of your desire to gossip, and so you are going to walk away in order to stick to your commitment.

2. Don't accuse the others who gossip. That only makes you self-righteous. Share your convictions for yourself and let others make up their own minds to do the same.

3. Stop the gossip. If you happen to hear some gossip about someone, tell the gossipers something like this: "I'm not sure that's true. Let's go ask her so we aren't gossiping." That will freak them out and they won't want you to do that, and that should be the end of that.

Don't Judge Others

As a person who knows God and his Word, you can find it very easy to judge others based on that knowledge. But to judge is to play God. You must judge for yourself what is good and what is sinful, but you cannot insult others for their actions. The God Girl doesn't say things in order to convict others but in order to love them. Conviction is God's job. The God Girl is never holier-than-thou; instead she is humble and thinks more highly of others than of herself. (Philippians 2:4) When she does this she entices people to know more about

"Before, you used to go
to this person and that,
but now the notion of
the Divine control
is forming so powerfully
in you that you go to
God about it."
Oswald Chambers

her and her God. Respect and an understanding that we all have sinned does more to draw people to the truth of God than a critical spirit ever could. God's Word makes it clear:

> Stop judging so that you will not be judged. Otherwise, you will be judged by the same standard you use to judge others. The standards you use for others will be applied to you. So why do you see the piece of sawdust in another believer's eye and not notice the wooden beam in your own eye? How can you say to another believer, "Let me take the piece of sawdust out of your eye," when you have a beam in your own eye? You hypocrite! First remove the beam from your own eye. Then you will see clearly to remove the piece of sawdust from another believer's eye.
>
> Matthew 7:1–5

Here are some things to put in your noggin when it comes to avoiding judging:

1. Be Switzerland. In the competition of life, choose to be neutral. Trust God to fight for you and protect you, and don't fight with others over their mistakes or problems.

2. Don't think too highly of yourself because of your successes. It's easy to judge others who don't have it together as much as you do. Everything you have is a gift from God, so don't become proud when you look at others who don't have as much.

3. Never compare yourself with others unless you are trying to make them look good. It's easy to judge others when you compare their lives to yours, so avoid it.

4. Don't be offended. It's easy to judge others when what they do or say offends you. But as a believer you don't have the right to be offended. Jesus is your model, and he was never offended for himself—only for his Father.

Control Your Emotions

The God Girl controls her emotions because she knows that emotions can sometimes be deceiving. When you always do what your emotions ask you to do, you lose. Emotions have no brain and they don't major in godliness. They can give great insight on things, and they are what makes you human, but they can't be in charge of what you say and do 24–7.

You have to remember that emotions come and go, and depending on what time of the month it is, emotions can be really destructive. When a girl wears her emotions on her sleeve, she forces other people to participate in them, and emotions can be contagious. God calls us to be joyful, to think positively, and to love others (see Psalm 19:14; Colossians 3:1–2). None of those involve dragging people into your emotional turmoil. So emotions have to be put

Connect the Branches

No branch is connected to another branch, except through the vine. So when you want to communicate with another branch, where you get in trouble is when you try to communicate branch-to-branch instead of going through the vine. That means that you have to communicate through Christ to reach another person. In other words, communicate in a Christlike manner. That means saying things without your own self-interest at heart and saying them in love.

When you look at a vine with many branches, you don't see the vine right away; you see all the branches. That's why it's doubly important that you represent the vine and draw in people who aren't a part of the vine, those branches scattered on the ground, through how you communicate. When a nonbeliever first sees you, they don't necessarily see you as a part of the entire plant, branches and vine. If you communicate in a godly way, you draw them closer to the vine, where God can graft them back into the vine. If a nonbeliever doesn't like the way you communicate, what then is going to attract them to the vine?

under the control of your mind. In the Bible we are warned to "keep away from worldly desires that wage war against your very souls" (1 Peter 2:11 NLT). Instead we are to "love each other" (John 15:17). So how do you control your emotions enough to communicate the way God wants you to communicate? It can take time and can seem almost impossible, but it can be done. Here's how to get started:

1. Don't feed your bad emotions. When you start to feel bad, take a look at your thoughts. What are you thinking about? If it's bad stuff, then change the subject to something good and get rid of those bad emotions.

2. Feed your good emotions. Think positive. Think about good things, happy things, godly things. And always run all your emotions by the Word of God. Are they consistent with his Word or arguing with it?

3. Don't make decisions or start big discussions when your emotions are crazy. You can control your emotions by not letting them control you. I know not to make any big decisions or start any major discussions when I have PMS because I know I can easily lose control.

Don't Argue or Fight

The God Girl doesn't argue or fight because she knows that "A servant of the Lord must not quarrel but must be kind to everyone, be able to teach, and be patient with difficult people" (2 Timothy 2:24 NLT). When you

A servant of the Lord must not quarrel but must be kind to everyone, be able to teach, and be patient with difficult people.
2 Tim. 2:24
NLT

fight with someone, you are out of control. Fighting simply means that what others think or do matters so much to you that you have to change them. And the truth is, what others do should never be so important to us that we argue or fight in order to change them. The God Girl knows that she can't change anyone but herself, so fighting is futile. It only makes her look out of control and angry, and it brings no glory to her God.

Don't let disagreement with those you love ever become an excuse to stop loving them. That is to deny God's law and to make up your own. The God Girl must love at all times, even when she is hurt or angry or disagrees with those she loves. It can be really hard to control yourself when you have the urge to fight, but when you do you build your character and you grow in strength. Proverbs 20:3 says, "Avoiding a quarrel is honorable. After all, any stubborn fool can start a fight." Don't be a stubborn fool. Let go and let God deal with the person, and you will show not only your love but also your undying trust in the God of the universe.

Control Your Tongue

> With our tongues we praise our Lord and Father. Yet, with the same tongues we curse people, who were created in God's likeness. Praise and curses come from the same mouth. My brothers and sisters, this should not happen! Do clean and polluted water flow out of the same spring?
>
> James 3:9–11

The God Girl uses her tongue to praise God, to worship him, to pray to him, and to love him. With it she gives hope to those around her and communicates love to those who will listen. Because of who she is and who she believes in, the God Girl doesn't want her tongue to ever get out of control. When it does she hurts not only her reputation but the reputation of the God she praises.

You can't be a God Girl and use your tongue for sin. That means you can't use it like a weapon, swinging it all around, knocking people in the head and the heart. You have to use it wisely. Control your urge to let loose on someone who has offended you or hurt you, and instead choose to use your mouth only for good, only for building up. "Don't say anything that would hurt [another person]. Instead, speak only what is good so that you can give help wherever it is needed. That way, what you say will help those who hear you" (Ephesians 4:29).

"I will watch my ways so that I do not sin with my tongue. I will bridle my mouth while wicked people are in my presence."

Psalm 39:1

Your tongue and the words you choose represent the God you serve. So choose them wisely. Here's how:

1. Don't get revenge. "Do not say, 'I'll get even with you!' Wait for the LORD, and he will save you." (Proverbs 20:22). When someone hurts you, insults you, or hates you, look to God for your hope. Taking vengeance doesn't get you what you want and only draws you further into pain and darkness. Obedience to God's Word in everything, especially in pain, will give you peace and hope. (See Deuteronomy 11:26-28; Proverbs 28:19.)

2. Don't brag (James 3:14). Never use your tongue to brag about yourself. It sounds awful to those who listen, and you lose any sign of being a God Girl.

3. Don't say anything out of jealousy (James 3:16). Jealousy is sinful. It doesn't help others; it only accuses God of not loving you enough to give you what He gave them.

You prove your love to God and to the world when you learn to control what you say. The God Girl knows that when she gets to heaven, she's going to have to give an account for every careless word she says (Matthew 12:36–37). Knowing that gives her the strength to communicate in love. She knows there is more at stake than just

being heard. She communicates love and hope, not bitterness and anger. When the God Girl enters a room, people don't run off or avoid her, because she is fun to be around. She uses her thoughts and her words to build up, to honor, and to respect, and in turn she is honored and respected herself.

When you trust God's Word instead of your own abilities to get what you want, and when you believe God hears your every thought and because of that other people don't have to hear everything you are thinking, you are free. Free to be who you were meant to be. Free from self-obsession and free from having to fight and scrap to get what you want. Learning to communicate in love will set you free to be the best God Girl you can be.

God Girl Checklist

Try silence—You can't listen while you are talking, so try this exercise. Find a weekend when you don't have work or a game or any other commitment, and make it your silent weekend. Tell your family and friends that you are not talking for

Obedience to God's Word in everything, especially in pain, will give you peace and hope.

forty-eight hours. Gulp! Can you do it? You might be surprised how it affects your thoughts, your communication, and your relationships. Give it a try and devote much of that time to reading and listening to God.

Practice listening—Think the first one was hard? Try this one if you are brave enough. The next time you talk to your friend, don't talk about yourself. Keep the conversation on her or on God. Every time it comes back to you, get back on track and talk about her, her feelings, her thoughts. Ask her questions. And if you really want to blow your parents' minds, try this on one of them too. They might think something is fishy, but don't give up; just don't talk about yourself. Afterwards, do a little journaling. Write about the experience—how hard it was, what you got out of it, and how the other person reacted.

Become a giver—One of the best ways to communicate the love of God with the world is by giving to the world where the world has need. So get involved in making the world a better place. Volunteer this month. Look around for a need and get involved. If you can't figure out where to start, get online and google "volunteer opportunities." You'll be able to find all kinds of things you can do in your city. Even if you live in a small town and there is nothing organized to help with, look around your neighborhood and help where you can. Carry groceries for your neighbor lady. Pick up trash at the park. Just don't let another month go by without giving back to the world.

5

A Girl Who Knows
Herself

All my life I wanted to be famous.

I loved performing, acting, dancing, singing, and I did all I could to make that my job. My goal was to go to LA and get a sitcom of my own. I loved acting and making people laugh more than anything. When I was in my twenties I started singing and got discovered by a producer and manager. I was so excited and dreamt of becoming a country music star.

I was sure my dream was coming true, until one day I was told I had to choose. I had to choose between singing and serving God on the college leadership at my church. It didn't seem like a fair question to ask, but as a new member of leadership I had to answer it: would I serve God or myself and my dream of fame?

I struggled with the question as I sat in my yellow convertible VW Bug and cried. But as I talked with God, I started to see that my passion for fame was getting in the way of my desire to get closer to God. So on the spot, I gave it all up. My lifelong dreams. Everything I had worked for. I gave it up then and there, all because I wanted to serve God more than I wanted anything else. But I believed him when he said he wanted only the best for me. And I believed that he would give me the desires of my heart (see Psalm 37:4).

Only a few years later, that belief proved to be true. I went from singing in bars and trying to get a record label to sign me to becoming a bestselling author who got to share God's hope with millions of people across the world. My love of making people laugh was not tossed away; it was just rearranged and made better by God himself.

Everyone has dreams, hopes, and fantasies about their life and who they want to be. It's part of growing up and making plans. You have to dream; you have to imagine your life as it could be. There is nothing wrong with that. In fact, it's the job of every God Girl to search herself and her God to discover what she was made for and what she will become. I believe who you can become has no limit other than God's limits. And that means that whatever he has planned for you will be amazing and more than you could ever imagine. "I know the plans that I have for you, declares the Lord.

I know the plans that I have for you, declares the Lord. They are plans for peace and not disaster, plans to give you a future filled with hope. Jer. 29:11

113

They are plans for peace and not disaster, plans to give you a future filled with hope" (Jeremiah 29:11). I lived off of this verse for many years. I was so sad when I had to give up my dreams, but I was also so certain that God would come through on his promise. And you have to be certain of that too. No matter what God has planned for you, it will blow your socks off if you are willing to be honest with yourself about who he's made you to be. That means that as a God Girl you have to know yourself: your weaknesses and your strengths, your abilities and your inabilities. You also have to know your danger zones: things you may be chasing after that promise success and hope but are only a cheap imitation of what God really wants for you.

God doesn't leave you to figure this stuff out on your own. He is right beside you, guiding you and talking to you, if you will only listen. But listening to God isn't always easy when the world is shouting in your ear. When you understand the way God guides you to your purpose, and when you can recognize the sound of his voice, you will more quickly see his plans for you and know where to go next in your journey of life. So let's take a look at some ways that you can get to know yourself better than you do right now.

Know Your Weaknesses

It can be easy to ignore your weaknesses or to say that you don't have any, but that is never true. We are all weak in different areas. And those weaknesses should not be feared but recognized (see 2 Corinthians 12:7-10). Being honest about what you can and can't do, where you are weak and where you are strong, is the quickest way to get into line with God's will for your life. Because when you deceive yourself or you let others lie to you, you miss out on the true gifts that are right in front of you.

Weaknesses don't have to be bad things. When you own them and refuse to let them get you down or lie to you anymore, they can be the very thing that gets you to the feet of Jesus. That's because without weakness you wouldn't need him. So let's take a look at a few signs that point to your weaknesses. See if any of these are showing up in your life. Then thank God for showing them to you.

Guilt

The guilt I'm talking about here is the guilt you feel when you do something wrong. It's a feeling that comes over you when what you do and what you believe don't line up. For a believer, guilt isn't a bad thing; it isn't punishment, for there is no condemnation for those who are in Christ (see Romans 8:1). But it is a sense of knowing, a nudge in your heart that something is wrong, and that's why feelings of guilt need to be listened to—not fretted over or stewed over but soberly listened to.

When you feel guilty, you have to determine if it's because of some sin in your life that you haven't given up or confessed. If it is, you have to stop that sin right away.

Sin is **weakness;**

It is the best way to get you away from your purpose. It makes you

unsure,

unstable,

and undirected.

In order to know who you truly are, you have to be willing to **be honest with yourself** about what makes you feel guilty and then have the strength of will to stop the action that leads you there.

Because guilt can be so hard to read—is it real guilt or false guilt?—it's important to find someone who can help you know the difference. Every God Girl should have a mentor or a discipler, someone who knows God's Word and is brave enough to point out your weaknesses and sin yet compassionate enough to help you through the rough parts of life.

After you identify the sin in your life that is causing all your guilt and you confess it to God with the intention of never doing that thing again, you can be sure that you are no longer guilty (see Psalm 32:5). If you continue to feel guilty after confession and repentance, then you are living a lie. The lie is that God isn't big enough to forgive *you,* as if you are some special case.

The Vinedresser

In the vineyard, the vinedresser finds sick vines. Those are the ones that have fallen to the ground and are covered in dirt and mold. These vines can't produce any fruit living down in darkness, so the vinedresser lifts them up and cleans them off. He doesn't chop them off, but he lifts them up so that they can get into the sunlight and start to produce fruit. They are valuable to him and may still be able to be productive when he gets them up off the ground.

From a spiritual perspective, your sin is what makes you sick and dirty and unable to bear fruit. And when that happens God, the vinedresser, comes along and shakes your world. He scrubs and cleans and moves you to another place.

Do you have some stuff in your past that you have given up—bad stuff, sinful stuff that you have moved past? If you can look back and see a change has come to your life, then you are bearing fruit. The light is coming to you and growth is happening. If you can't look back and see how your life has changed, then maybe it's time to start paying attention to the hand of God in your life. Find out where he's trying to clean you up and lift you up, and stop fighting him.

He could forgive murderers, prostitutes, and thieves, but not you. See the lie? When you confess and repent you can be sure that you are no longer guilty, and any feeling of guilt you have did not and will never come from God. When you understand God's power to forgive then you have freedom—freedom to be who you were made to be, without all the chains of spiritual confusion and deception. Finding the feelings of guilt in your life instead of ignoring them will help you to better know not only yourself but your God as well. Here's how to start dealing with the guilt in your life:

1. Listen. When you read a book like this or hear something someone else says and it makes you feel guilty—listen. God could be talking to you.

2. Investigate the pain. If something is giving you emotional pain, pay attention to it. Could God be trying to talk to you to get you to see where you are sinning? Not all emotional pain is a sign of guilt, but it's a good place to investigate your holy health. It could be a sign of God's holy discipline (Proverbs 3:11).

3. Don't ignore the silence. You can't find more of God if you are ignoring his discipline or his law. Silence in your study time might just mean there is something you need to confess and to get rid of. Take some time to figure out what that could be (Psalm 66:18).

4. Get over it. If you have examined your guilt in the light of God's Word and agreed with him by confessing what needs to be confessing and promising not to do it again then the guilt is gone. No more guilt. That means you've got to get over it. Holding onto your guilt is denying the gift of God.

Drama

Another thing that points to weakness in your life is drama. Think about the drama in your past or your present. What did it center around? How did you react? How did you feel? Drama isn't healthy; it doesn't point to a girl set on pleasing God but a girl who has lost her way a little bit. Drama is a sign of weakness, because it is in weakness that you allow things of this world to become more important than they are. Nothing should be so important as to cause you drama.

In order to be honest with your-self about who you are and who God made you to be, you have to identify the problem with drama. You have to recog-nize what causes it in your life, and the answer can't be them or her. It has to be something inside of your-self. What is it in you that makes you react the way you do? What makes you

care the way you care? Where is God in the drama? What are his thoughts on your thoughts? And why are your emotions allowed to rule over God's law?

The God Girl knows who she is—a child of God, not a child of her whims, her fears, or her anger. If you are prone to drama, one way to avoid it is to do the opposite of what your inclination is. Look for drama and go the other direction. If your instinct is to freak out, then do the opposite. Open up your Bible and read. Get out a piece of paper and journal. Talk to someone who is calm. If your instinct is to argue, then shut up. If you tend to cry, then laugh. Do the opposite in order to get yourself out of the drama rut. Don't let drama distract you from the more important things in life, but use what you know about your own drama to draw you closer to God instead of closer to the problem that got the drama going in the first place. Here's how you can handle the temptation to drama like a true God Girl:

1. Ask yourself this question every time drama pops up: "Am I saying this now to win the approval of people or God? Am I trying to please people? If I were still trying to please people, I would not be Christ's servant" (Galatians 1:10).

2. Learn to die to self. God calls us to die to our sinful nature, not to listen to it anymore. Anything that causes drama is sin. So look for the sin in your heart that is leading to the drama (see Galatians 5:19–21).

3. Become a peacemaker. "God blesses those who work for peace, for they will be called the children of God" (Matthew 5:9 NLT). Look for ways to create peace, not drama.

Repeated Failure

Failure is not sure sign of weakness. Edison failed over 10,000 times before inventing the lightbulb. Failure is a necessary part of life, but failure can also be a sign that you are going the wrong direction. If there is something you keep trying but you keep failing at, take a long hard look at yourself. Are you being honest with yourself? Are others saying you should give up what it is you keep failing at? Is God trying to get you to turn around and try another door? Don't let failure get you down, but use it for your good. Either you will grow stronger in the face of it and

The God Girl knows who she is— a child of God, not a child of her whims, her fears, or her anger.

You don't have to
feel good
to be
godly.

continue till you succeed, or you will take it as evidence that you don't know yourself well enough and it's time to start looking for more insight from God on where to go next. Here are some ideas for you when failure is a part of your life:

1. Get a second opinion. Failure isn't always bad; sometimes it's good practice for success. But if all you ever do is fail, then maybe it's time to get a second opinion. Ask someone who is smart, wise, and godly if they think you could ever be great at what you are failing at right now. If they say no, then maybe you are seeking something that wasn't intended for you (see Proverbs 12:15).

2. Get God's help. If you continue to fail at something, spend some time—not just fifteen minutes but hours—seeking God about your strengths and what he wants you to do with your life. Ask him to open a door for you in this area if it is his will. One door might just be all you need to keep going, but if no doors open, then maybe it's time to move on to some other dream.

Obsession

A surefire way to spot your weaknesses is to look at what you think about the most. Wherever you have an obsession, you have a pretty good chance of finding a weakness. Obsession leads to weakness because it distracts you from God. Anything that takes up that much of your mind space saps your spiritual and emotional strength. When you can't be honest with yourself about what you obsess over, you run the risk of being controlled by the very thing you crave. Man cannot serve two masters—God and anything else. If he tries, he'll end up hating one of them (see Matthew 6:24). And who do you think it will be? So know what obsesses you and call it what it is: a weakness. Then do what you can walk away from it and toward God.

Not sure what you are obsessed about? Here are a few questions to get you thinking:

1. What do you think about the most?
2. What is one thing you could never live without?
3. What keeps you up at night?
4. What worries you the most?
5. What are you afraid of?
6. What do you get in trouble for the most?

Now think about your answers and consider which of these might be your obsession. Do any of them get in the way of time with God? Do any of them lead you to sin? Remember, sin can be something like worry, fear, doubt, anger, bitterness, revenge, or hate. If there is anything you can't give up, you have an obsession. Anything that causes you to sin is an obsession and has to be given up. So think about your list and pray about it. Then make some decisions today!

Busyness

Being busy can be fun. It makes you feel alive and active. But being busy can also be a sign of weakness, and distraction from what's really important. In the parable of the vine and the branches, Jesus talks about how the vinedresser, God, prunes the vines to make them healthy (see John 15:1–8). Pruning means cutting away the good things, things like leaves and even fruit, in order to help the branch grow more and better fruit. And spiritually the vinedresser, God, often cuts away the good things from your life. When your life gets too busy, when things and people become more important to you than God, you can find yourself in pain. Stress, anxiety, and fatigue can wear at you and distract you from being your best. When too much crowds your life, you can sometimes start to feel the hand of God pruning and cutting what needs to go in order to make you thrive.

A few years ago a dream of mine came true. I got asked to help create and speak on a major tour. I was so excited. It was something I had dreamt of since I was a kid, and now it had suddenly happened. I couldn't believe it. Things went well for a few weeks, and then it happened: they changed their minds, they dumped me, we "broke up." And my heart was broken. I didn't see it coming. I grieved. I couldn't understand why God would take away something so big and so important to my ministry. But then he showed me. A week later I got pregnant with my daughter Addy, and my life was forever changed. No matter how much I loved that tour and all it meant to me, I wouldn't change having Addy for anything. See, if I had kept on touring, we wouldn't have tried to have a baby, because we would have been too busy for such a thing. God knew that, and I am so very glad that he sacrificed the good for the best in my life.

Is your life too full? Do you run from event to event—practice, clubs, meetings, ministering, attending, studying, and on and on? A life that is too full can squeeze out time for God. And if you let it go too long, he's going to start pruning. So when things feel overwhelming and stressful, stop and take a listen. Have you crowded out the vine and any chance for you to produce a whole bunch more fruit? If so, try these tips to help you get the busyness under control:

1. God time. The best way to beat busyness is to commit to spending time in prayer and study each morning before you leave the house. The more time the better. It might seem like you don't have time for God because you have too many other things to do, but think about that statement. You can't do anything without him, and you can do all things with him. So if you are too busy, then slow down and take some time to get with God.

2. Learn to say no. Saying no isn't being lazy, and it isn't sinful. No just means that you have other things to do that you consider more important. You don't have to say yes to everything people ask you to do in order to be godly. It doesn't make you godly; it just makes you busy. Remember, if becoming too busy causes you to sin, then you have to stop the busy and learn to say no.

Knowing Yourself, Showing Yourself

Once you know yourself, you have to show yourself. The God Girl is always consistent. She is the same on the outside as she is on the inside, and that's why the world sees in her just who she is. She doesn't misrepresent herself or her God. That means her look, her style, her attitude, and her words all express her faith. If you are a God Girl, you will be the same in all these areas.

Style

How you dress tells others who you are. Is your wardrobe consistent with your beliefs? How does God feel about your clothes? What does your style do to the guys around you? Do you lead guys into temptation with your body, your cleavage, your thighs? These questions might sound old-fashioned and unfair, but the truth is that a God Girl understands that her life isn't her own. She lives to love God and to love others, and because of that she doesn't ever want to become a stumbling block for anyone (see 1 Corinthians 8:9). She lives not to feel good about her clothes but to glorify God, and so before she walks out of the house each day, she checks herself: "Am I revealing parts of me that turn guys on?" It's a simple question but one that a girl who is honest with herself about who she is and who God wants her to be will willingly answer. Your style and your body represent God. Is he proud of you or unhappy?

This should give you freedom. It means that you don't have to dress to keep up with the world. It means that you can have your own style. And it means that your

A God Girl lives to love God and to love others, and because of that she doesn't ever want to become a stumbling block for anyone.

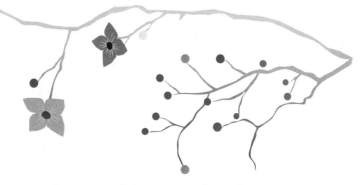

measure of cute isn't how new and trendy you are but how holy and kind you are. If you struggle with what to wear and how to glorify God, you aren't alone. Me and a million other girls are right there with you. So take heart, but also take time to find out how to fix things.

Not sure if your clothes are messing with the guys around you? Think about these Qs:

1. Have you ever been called a tease?
2. Do boys stare at your chest when they talk to you?
3. When you bend over in front of a mirror, do you see more than you realized?

If you want more help with your wardrobe, check out *Sexy Girls: How Hot Is Too Hot?* or *Hotness: A PB&J Bible Study*.

In Love with Being in Love

You know that yummy feeling you get in the pit of your stomach when you are in love? You know how the

"If through a broken
heart God can bring His
purposes to pass in the world,
then thank Him
for breaking your heart."
Oswald Chambers

world looks brighter, the birds sing louder, and your heart is happier? Being in love has got to be one of the most amazing things that can ever happen. It's a drug; it gives your body a high, setting off all kinds of endorphins that make you feel invincible. Love is so amazing that a lot of times it can become an addiction. When that happens you fall in love with the feeling of being in love. And while the feelings of love aren't bad, to be in love with them, rather than actually in love with the person, is a messed-up kind of love. And it can do all kinds of things to your heart and mind.

When you are in love with being in love, you do stupid things. You settle for **stupid love** rather than real, genuine, and **true love**. See, true love doesn't always feel good. It sometimes requires you to give up things you want and to do things you don't want. It is sacrificial, as seen in the life of Christ, and it doesn't always feel good. When you are in love with love, you miss out on the true purpose of love, and you become all about feelings and less about action.

If you notice that you have to have a guy in your life in order to feel happy, then you might just be in love with being in love. Feeling love should never be your goal, but giving love should be.

If you are in love with being in love, then it's time to get your love life straightened out. Consider these facts about love and look at the love you crave to see how it compares:

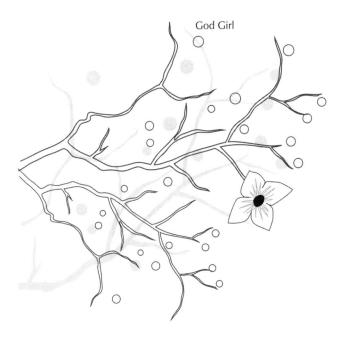

1. Love doesn't get mad when it doesn't get what it wants.
2. Love isn't jealous.
3. Love isn't happy when other people grovel.
4. Love doesn't require good feelings.
5. Love keeps no record of wrong.
6. Love isn't "all about me."
7. Love is selfless.
8. Love doesn't make demands.

Getting Physical

A God Girl knows herself, and she knows that looking for loopholes in God's commandments is a slippery

so afraid of what to say and how to say it. But when I started to speak and write books, my life changed. Suddenly people I'd never met or seen knew who I was. I didn't know them, but they sure knew me. And because of that, if I ignore anyone, I look like a meanie. After all, they feel like they know me. So in order to overcome my shyness, I just pretend like everyone knows me and I have to talk to them. It's really helped me to break my cycle and to risk talking to people.

So when you are around new people, smile and say "hi" like it's good to see them again. Never assume you don't know them, but pretend like you do and you just can't remember where from. You don't want to be mean, and so you just say hi to everyone. When given the chance ask them how they are. Engage them as if they are super shy and really want to talk to you but will never start anything. Help them out. Pretend like you are super confident and want to help people to feel

135

at home. When you think of yourself as a missionary, reaching out to people in need, instead of a new person in need yourself, you will have the strength and confidence to do what only really confident people do.

2. Rehearse. Not sure what to say to strangers? Well, do some rehearsal. Write down some nice things to say to people—compliments, one-liners, jokes, things that would make people feel good—and memorize them. Practice them. Don't let shyness beat you—show it who's boss!

Know Your Strengths

As a God Girl it's important to know yourself well enough to not only know your strengths but also to act on them. Just like that little light of yours, your strengths can't be hidden under a bushel. You have to let them out, let them shine, and let them do what they gotta do. Jesus talks about not wasting your gifts and opportunities when he tells the story about the talents (see Matthew 25:14–30).

Your talents might be totally obvious or they might be in hiding, but either way I can tell you for sure that you have some, no matter how lost you might feel at times. But don't worry; there is hope. When you are searching for yourself, your dreams, and your future, you can do some things that will help you drill down to what's important so that you can make steps in the right direction for you. I've always loved that part of life—the exploring part. At this time in your life you have more possibilities than you will ever have again. The world is yours to explore.

I remember a time when I was trying to find my way from Portland, Oregon, to anywhere else in the world. I wanted a change, and I wanted to make a difference. I felt there was a call on my life to do work that was also ministry. I wasn't happy any more just putting soles on people's feet (I worked in the shoe industry); I wanted to change their souls. One of the things I did that really helped me to figure out my strengths and my weaknesses was to take some personality tests. There are a ton of them out there, like the Myers-Briggs inventory and others, and you can get many of them free online. As you take them you will find out a ton about yourself and hopefully get some info on the way your future will unfold.

If there is something that you think you'd just love to do, think about finding an internship in that area to see if you really like it once you actually do it. Or try out job shadowing. Do whatever you can to get the information you need to make a good decision about what you want to, or need to, do with your life.

For me, work in ministry was what I really wanted. I just couldn't see myself doing anything other than God stuff all day. But I wasn't sure that meant working at a church or anything like that. So I had to explore. I had two great options. A church in Hawaii actually wanted me to start a singles group for them. Talk about paradise, huh?

And then there was publishing. Thomas Nelson wanted me to work for them making books for Christians. Both sounded good, but I had no idea which to choose. So I took lots of tests and talked to lots of people. I finally got an answer I liked from someone who told me, "When choosing between two good things, feel free to choose what compels you—what you really, really want." And for some odd reason I really wanted publishing, and I actually passed up Hawaii. Crazy, I know, but hey, it seems to have worked out for me, so I guess I did good.

If there is something that you love and are really good at, then you can consider doing it as ministry. Want to be a doc? Then how about going to a country that needs you and serving the poor there? Want to build houses? How about finding a ministry that builds homes for needy people? You can do so many things with your talents, but the one thing you can't do is let them go to waste. So do the work it takes to find out where you can invest the gifts God has given you so that your life will be more than you ever dreamt it could be!

God Girl Checklist

Check yourself—Find out if who you think you are is who the world thinks you are. Answer these questions: What are my biggest weaknesses? What are my biggest strengths? Then ask three other people who know you well how they would answers these same questions about you, and then see if there is agreement. If they don't agree with you, take some time to figure out why. Who is right and who is wrong?

Do a self-assessment—Is there anything you've been doing for a long time that leaves you feeling bad, guilty, or stressed? If so, it might be time to call it what it is: a distraction from the main thing, or even a sin. Don't let your busy life crowd out what really counts. So get a piece of paper and write down some things that you think might be things that God wants you to remove from your life. If they are sin or are leading you to sin, then cut them out.

Rebuke review—Think about your life over the past five years. Can you remember any rebukes God has sent your way? Any things you were doing that he took away or that you gave up willingly? Think about why and about how much your life has changed since then. Then spend some time thanking God for his love and discipline.

Action inventory—Not sure if your actions are consistent with who you are? Then do an action inventory. Look at the areas of your life below and write down your actions. Need help? Ask your friends how you act in these areas. Then write down how that compares with who you really are. If you find inconsistencies, then it's time to make some changes. Do your research, read books that help you better understand who God wants you to be, and hopefully you'll get to the bottom of who you want to be and who you were made to be.

Wardrobe—Does your wardrobe reflect your faith? (For more study on this issue, check out *Sexy Girls: How Hot Is Too Hot?*)

Friendship—Are there people who hate you, who are afraid of you, or who you hate? (Need more info on this? Read *Mean Girls: Facing Your Beauty Turned Beast*.)

Boys—How do you interact with boys? What kinds of things do you do with them? (Look at *Technical Virgin: How Far Is Too Far?* for tons of insight on this topic.)

Faith—Do you walk the talk? How does your faith look from the outside? Interview your friends and ask them what they think about your faith. (Have a look at *Idol Girls: What's Your Obsession?* for help on getting your faith right on the outside and inside.)

Talk—How do you talk? Do you cuss? Are you a complainer, or are you critical? How do your words line up with what you believe?

6

A Girl Who Knows God

To be a God Girl is an amazing thing. It means that God, the Creator of the universe, the all-powerful, all-knowing King of Kings, has adopted you as his own. He has made you his daughter, his little girl, and he is your Father. Think about that for a moment. It's an incredible position, one that wipes out every other amazing thing in the world with it's super-duper amazingness.

When I first found out about who God was and how much he loved me despite my messed-up life, I couldn't contain myself. I can remember putting on songs about Jesus on the cross and about him giving up everything for me, and I sobbed. I was overwhelmed with the magnitude of the gift of salvation. My life before Christ was filled with angst, anger, loneliness, isolation, fear, worry, and depression. Sure, I had moments of happiness, but they were so precarious, so dependent on circumstances, that they easily tumbled and left me in the rubble. So when I looked to Jesus, the Rock, the one who never changes, never leaves, and never stops loving, I fell to the floor in relief. It was like a load was lifted off my back. I wasn't in charge of my destiny. I wasn't lost and alone in darkness; I was connected to him who loves. I was loved, and it was an incredible feeling.

You too are loved. No matter what you've done. No matter what! Nothing you have done in the past can keep you from the love of God. Nothing. You are on his heart. He smiles when he sees you, and he waits for your next glance in his direction and for your words of affection and trust. But he isn't a big teddy bear just waiting passively for your next hug; he is a powerful and perfect God who won't tolerate sin in your life. And that knowledge a lot of the time becomes our sole focus. That's why balance is important in the life of the God Girl. You have to be willing to agree with God that sin isn't good for you or for the world, and then you have to accept the love that he freely gives when you turn to him. It's a beautiful relationship, really. God gives you beautiful boundaries—boundaries that keep you from falling off the cliff or bumping into the electric fence.

When you choose God by accepting his outstretched hand and holding on for dear life, things change. Maybe not all at once, but over time your life gets better. Sure, things are bound to go wrong. People will distract you, toys will entice you, and you will look away from the one who gives you life, but there is always a way back. And even if you haven't walked away from God, I hope you will always want more of him. More hope, more peace, more love, and more faith.

The good thing is that God has made a way for you. He has given you what you need to find him and what you need to stay near him. It's just that sometimes you get off track and you need some help getting back to the basics. So how do you come to know him more? How do you keep your focus off of your problems and on your God? Let's have a look.

A God Girl Prays

We are confident that God listens to us if we ask for anything that has his approval. We know that he listens to our requests. So we know that we already have what we ask him for.

1 John 5:14–15

Are you confident that God is listening? Does he pay attention to your cry? Is he waiting to meet your needs? How has your prayer life been? Could it be

"I praise the word of God.

I trust God.

I am not afraid.

What can mere flesh
[and blood] do to me?"

Psalm 56:4

better? Prayer is something that sets the life of the God Girl apart from the rest of the world. She converses with the God of the universe and he listens. How amazing is that? Prayer is your all-access pass to the Father, and because of it your life is sweeter and more hopeful.

Without prayer you couldn't call yourself a God Girl. You can't love a person and refuse to talk to them. Talking bonds you. It's how you share your hearts. You talk, you listen, and you bond. You get closer and you get to know each other. Prayer is your talking with God. And it's what changes your life from ordinary to amazing.

But prayer isn't a given. It isn't always natural. Sometimes it can feel like work. Sometimes your mind wanders and your focus is drawn back to remembering past conversations with people, or planning your day, or worrying about the future. And when that happens, prayer can feel more like an obligation than a reward. But without prayer, your life will be bumpy. It will be messy; it will get all wadded up and blurry. It will become out of control and dirty. Prayer draws you back to the greater purpose; it reminds you who you are and who God is.

According to God's Word, prayer should be an integral part of your life. In fact, you are supposed to pray continually (see 1 Thessalonians 5:17). Wow, sound impossible? Crazy even? Well, it's actually not. Think it about it like this: prayer is your mind being hooked up to God's. It's always remembering he is closer to you than your own skin and never forgetting how much he cares and how much he can do in the life of a girl who will let him. God promises to listen to the ones who love him. "He listens to people who are devout and who do what he wants" (John 9:31). And you can also be sure that if you live in him and what he says lives in you, then you can ask for anything you want, and it will be yours (see John 15:7).

Yep, prayer is your connection to the Creator of the world. But sometimes that very fact can make it seem impossible. What do you say? How do you talk? Does he listen? The amazing thing is yes, he does. He listens to his people. And if you're a God Girl, that's you. But prayer requires a few things of you. Check it out.

He listens to people who are devout and who do what he wants.

John 9:31

Prayer Requires Faith

You can't pray to a God you don't believe in. That would be insanity. So you have to believe he is who he says he is. If you don't, then you can be sure he isn't listening. "No one can please God without faith. Whoever goes to God must believe that God exists and that he rewards those who seek him" (Hebrews 11:6).

Prayer Requires Godly Motives

God knows all your thoughts. He knows your motives—why you ask for what you ask for—so there's no pulling the wool over his eyes. When it comes to asking God for things, your heart has to be set on godliness, not your own wants. Prayers can go unanswered for all kinds of reasons, but one of them could be that what you are asking for isn't something that you want in order to know God more or to draw closer to him but is something you want to get or do to make yourself feel good. Think about some of the things you ask for. Are you asking for them so they can make you happy or complete? Isn't that God's job? Consider why you ask for things, and then focus on the things that please God—the things that make your relationship better rather than your life more fun. "When you pray for things, you don't get them because you want them for the wrong reason—for your own pleasure" (James 4:3).

Prayer Requires Patience

King David knew prayer. He was always praying, always calling out to God to help him and protect him,

"God is faithful and reliable. If we confess our sins, he forgives them and cleanses us from everything we've done wrong."

1 John 1:9

so you could say that he was experienced in the stuff of prayer. He knew that prayers weren't always answered on his timeline, so he was patient. David wrote, "I waited patiently for the LORD. He turned to me and heard my cry for help" (Psalm 40:1). That patience came out of an understanding that God would get to it when it was best gotten to.

For years and years I wanted God to answer my cry for love. I wanted to find the man who would never leave me. And I couldn't understand why God didn't seem to be listening. It wasn't until years later that I fully understood that I wasn't ready for love and neither was my man. Time had to do its work. I could have rushed God and took charge of things for myself and married the wrong guy. But I didn't. I waited till he and I were both ready, and because of that I was rewarded with the perfect man for me. Prayer requires patience, and patience comes from a belief that God has everything under control, even my dreams and my hopes.

Prayer Requires Trust

Sometimes God answers your prayers with a big no. But no isn't a bad thing when it comes from God. Nothing bad comes from God. So you can be sure that when you pray and God doesn't answer the way you want, something better is coming. "Glory belongs to God, whose power is at work in us. By this power he can do infinitely more than we can ask or imagine"

(Ephesians 3:20). As a God Girl you can know beyond a shadow of a doubt that God has only the best planned for you.

When I first came to know Christ, my favorite verse was Jeremiah 29:11. I read it every day; I wrote it everywhere; I needed to believe it. My life depended on it. Maybe it can bring some hope to you too: "I know the plans that I have for you, declares the LORD. They are plans for peace and not disaster, plans to give you a future filled with hope." If you can trust God's words, then you can trust him with your prayers, no matter what the answer.

Prayer Requires Confession

A girl first comes to know God through becoming aware that she isn't perfect, that she's messed up and needs the God who forgives to breathe life into her. At that moment the clouds open up and things start to become clearer. Confession—agreeing with God that he is right and your sin is wrong—brings a sigh of relief. It can be embarrassing and hard to get to the point of confessing your messed-up stuff, but once you can get it out and get through it, you find such relief.

At one time in my life I was a big, dirty, cloudy mess. I was stressed, depressed, worried, and obsessed with a boy who wasn't obsessed with me. I was in a spiritual dungeon, a place I put myself with all the stupid things I had done before I knew Christ. I can remember deciding to come clean and confess everything evil that I had ever done. I went to my youth pastor and I asked him and his wife for help. I needed to be free from my sin. And so we did it. We all sat in a room and I talked. I spilled it all. I confessed everything awful that I had done over my entire life. We left no stone unturned. We opened it all to the light. I remember that it was like my heart was a dark room filled with cockroaches of sin, and when I turned on the light of confession, they all scampered away, afraid of being seen and killed. Through the process of coming clean, my heart became clean. I didn't let darkness hide my sin any longer; I exposed it to the light of Christ and I was healed.

At that point my life changed forever. The nagging guilt I'd lived with for so many years went away. The fear of loneliness was wiped away. The worry, the stress—all lifted. Confession cleans you. Confessing that you were wrong and God was right and that you want to make him the Lord of your life is what first brings you to salvation. Without confession you wouldn't be a God Girl.

The daily practice of confession will keep you on track. When every morning you wake up and get real with God, when you don't hide anything, when you

2 Things God Won't Do When You Sin:

- discipline you just to be mean or spiteful or because life has been going too good for you and now it's time for some discipline
- hurt someone else to teach you a lesson—ever!

3 Things God Will Do When You Sin:

- discipline you when you do something wrong
- do what he can to show you your mistakes in order to get you out of the darkness
- accept your apology every time, anytime, forever

agree that you've done this and this and this wrong, you get stronger and stronger. Sin doesn't like to hang around when it knows that it's going to get ratted on. As a God Girl, you should make confession part of your daily routine so you're regularly getting everything out and agreeing with God that it was wrong. Confession is the beginning of prayer; it is a cleaning of the slate. So find time each day to be honest with God and with yourself. This is the start of knowing God and yourself and drawing your heart into a more holy life.

Prayer Requires Adoration

My prayer life was getting boring. I was doing the same thing every morning: going down my list of people and things to pray for and about. I was talking to God about me, and it was flat. Then Michael told me a way to pray that he learned in college. I tried it and it worked. And when I say it worked, I mean it changed my life. Not only did my prayers get better but my life got better. I got happier. And it was all because I start out every morning in adoration.

I focus all my mind on adoring God. I look out at the trees and see what an amazing artist he is. I thank him for his beauty, his power, his kindness. I just ooze love all over him. I can't stop talking about how incredible he is. You know how it feels when someone goes on and on about how amazing you are? It's so good. And I want God to feel good when we talk, so I go on and on about how great he is. I'm never at a loss. And as I verbally confirm what my heart has always known, I release everything awful and ugly from my life. I refocus on what is true and good, and I am drawn into his majesty. I become a part of his whole. Peace pours over me and I pour my love over him.

Adoration will give wings to your prayer life and your walking-around life. I know from experience that when I skip adoration, my day will be unhappy. My focus will be off, and I won't find my groove. But when I start the day with adoration, I can't contain my excitement. It fills my veins like adrenaline, and I am giddy. Life is good when you remember and say out loud that God is good too.

Prayer Requires Worship

"Holy, holy, holy is the Lᴏʀᴅ of Armies! The whole earth is filled with his glory."

Isaiah 6:3

155

"Every good present and every perfect gift comes from above, from the Father who made the sun, moon, and stars. The Father doesn't change like the shifting shadows produced by the sun and the moon."

James 1:17

When you worship God, you get outside of your-self. Your problems and your worries all become min-iscule compared to the **amazing power and love of God.** Worship gives God what he deserves: your undying attention and adoration.

Worship doesn't have to be about music, but most of the time that's what people think of. With music that expresses the goodness and power of God, you are drawn into worship and come closer to God than to any other human on earth.

The **God Girl** is different from the rest of the world because of who she worships. Your salvation, your eternity rests on the fact that you worship God and his Son Jesus Christ.

My prayer life is set to soar when I wake up and put on my favorite worship songs. As I sing the words that express his greatness, I am lifted out of the everyday life and raised up to a higher view of things. And it is in that worship that I can truly express to God how important he is to me.

But worship doesn't require music. You can worship God by just doing what he asks you do to. **Obedi-ence is worship.** You can worship him by serving others, by refusing to break and give in to the world. **Worship is more than just tunes; it's your lifestyle**—what you do each day with the fact that Jesus died on the cross for you.

Prayer Requires Thanksgiving

Make it a regular part of your day to give God thanks for all the good things in your life.

Another way to get your prayer and your life back on track with God is to get thankful. It's impossible to be thankful and depressed at the same time. Thankfulness is freedom. Complaining is bondage. It ties you down to the cares of this world and distracts you from true beauty. Make it a regular part of your day to give God thanks for all the good things in your life. Nothing is too mundane or silly. Everything you have that is good is from him, so thank him for it.

Prayer is an amazing thing. It gives life to your soul and freedom to your mind. Accept prayer as your daily devotion to God, your proof that he is yours and you are his, the branch of his vine, and you will be a true God Girl. Prayer isn't something that you perfect in one day, however; it takes a lifetime to learn its power and its ways. So take slow, deliberate steps and keep your eye on him, and you won't falter. And if you do, then just get back up again and back into conversation with the one true God.

A God Girl Is Saved by Grace

I can remember looking at all the sin in my life and feeling ashamed. I was bothered by all the missteps and bad choices I made. And I can also remember finding relief in the words of God. In fact, in the back of my Bible I wrote the word *relief*, and by it I wrote down every verse that made me feel better. It's an astounding thing to think about, but all your sin is forgivable. It is all covered under the grace of God. And because of that, you can be a confident God Girl who fearlessly walks into his presence, talks with him, shares her heart and her mind, and listens to everything the Father has to say.

Consider these words written to you:

But because of his great love for ~~us~~ you, God, who is rich in mercy, made ~~us~~ you alive with Christ even when ~~we~~ you were dead in transgressions—it is by grace you have been saved.

Ephesians 2:4–5 NIV

Grace reaches down and says, "I don't care how ugly, mean, or sinful you are or how bad you've been—I love you and if you will confess your mess-ups and then accept my forgiveness, it will be yours." Grace removes the stains from your life and makes you pure again.

My darling girl, God loved you before you were lovable, and he loved you enough to do the

Grace: the dimension of divine activity that enables God to confront human indifference and rebellion with an inexhaustible capacity to forgive and to bless. God is gracious in action.

Tyndale Bible Dictionary

unthinkable. "He who did not spare his own Son, but gave him up for us all—how will he not also, along with him, graciously give us all things?" (Romans 8:32–33 NIV). You can expect nothing but the best from God. When times look dark, when prayers seem unanswered, you have to hold on tight to the fact that **God has it covered.** He won't let anyone pull you from his hands, and he knows that you can handle everything that he allows to happen to you. Through trusting in that fact and refusing to doubt it, you will be able to overcome even the most heinous of circumstances. **God's grace is enough.**

A God Girl Studies

The God Girl is the luckiest girl in the world, because she doesn't have a hidden God or a dead God but has a living God who is willing and eager to communicate with her. Through prayer and the acceptance of his grace and forgiveness she can get closer to him, but one thing gets her even closer: studying his Word, the Bible. When you open up your Bible and start to read the words in it, they come to life. You can read it over and over again, and each reading gives you just what you need to improve your spirit and your mind.

Before I trusted Christ for my salvation, when I used to read the Bible it all sounded like Greek to me. I literally couldn't understand any of it. I tried and tried, but none of it made sense. And that was infuriating. But after I dedicated my life to him and to getting to know him more, it was like a veil was lifted off the pages and suddenly I could understand all of it. I was like a kid in the biggest toy store ever seen. A surprise was around every corner, and I couldn't get enough.

When you really want to know God, you've got to study. I mean you've got to—your mind won't let you rest till you do. You crave the answers, the truth about life, and so you study. But studying can get tough after a time. You've read it all before, and now you don't know what to do next, or you can't decide where to start. Studying doesn't come naturally to all of us, and although you really want to know more about God, you might not know how to go about it. So let me help you out with some ways I've succeeded in discovering the truth in God's Word on a daily basis.

The goal—The goal for your study time should be to find out more about the God you love. Find out what he likes and dislikes and how he acts, sounds, and interacts. When all you want to know is who he is and what he wants, your study time becomes a lot more directed and manageable.

Research—For me, the best time in study is the time when I am researching a book. I have a topic all picked out, like idolatry or mean or sex. Whatever the topic is, I start to research all that God has to say about it. I open up a concordance or look up the topic online or in my Bible software, and I start to climb. I move from one verse to the next, and then that takes me to an-other idea that is connected to my main topic. As I work I write down what I am learning. I write small paragraphs on each topic and fill them out with a bunch of verses that support the idea. I work to make a case for whatever it is I am researching. As I do, the Bible starts to come to life, and so does my study time. It's as if the Bible is a bottomless cave of priceless gems and experiences. I can never draw all there is to draw out of it. If you want your study to come to life, consider drilling into a topic as I do when I write a book. It will help you to learn more than you ever knew and to stay focused on the job at hand.

The tools—In order to really dive into Bible study, you have to have the tools needed. First is a good translation. Consider one that you can understand easily, something readable like the GOD'S WORD translation or the New Living Translation. Something that makes sense to you. Then find some reference works like a Bible handbook or a concordance. If you don't have them at home, you can always look online for Bible tools like an online concordance or a searchable Bible. You can also just type the topic you are studying into your search engine and see what you can find. But bring it all back to your Bible. Don't take other people's word for it. Find out how what they are saying lines up with Scripture. And if you still aren't sure, keep researching. Here are some sample sources (some free, some not) for your studying tools:

Strong's Concordance
Bible Knowledge Commentary
Believers Bible Commentary
New American Commentary
New Topical Textbook
Where to Find it in the Bible
Illustrated Manners and Customs
Any good Bible dictionary

You can also go to your pastor and find out what commentaries and reference works he uses.

When you want more of God—more of his grace, his peace, and his hope—you have to be willing to do some heavy lifting. You can't just wait for it to come to you through osmosis by sleeping with the Bible under your pillow. You have to be willing to do the work. Read the

"The initiative of the saint is not towards self-realization, but towards

knowing Jesus Christ.

The spiritual saint never believes circumstances to be haphazard, or thinks of his life as secular and sacred; he sees everything he is dumped down in as the means of securing the knowledge of Jesus Christ. There is a reckless abandonment about him."

Oswald Chambers

words, find out what you need to know, and don't rely on others. Sure, others can help guide you and get you started, but ultimately you are responsible for knowing why you believe what you believe. You are old enough and smart enough to do this. You can dive into God's Word like anyone else. You can find out what God wants of you and what would make him happy. You can feel closer to him and less stressed out by life if you will only open up his Word each day and do a little work. Read a little, search a little, learn your way around your faith, and your life will continue to improve.

The God Girl is a student of her God. She takes nothing for granted but seeks to find out who he is and how he loves. The God Girl stays connected to God through prayer and study. She worships him freely, adores him, and agrees with him when she messes up. The God Girl knows herself because she knows the God who created and purposed her for good works. She communicates in love and knows the secret to true happiness is found in loving him. And she finds love abundantly because she sees the world through God's eyes. She

The God Girl takes nothing for granted but seeks to find out who he is and how he loves.

gives love—not to get it back but to share that which her God has given her. The God Girl is a breath of fresh air to a perishing world. She rises above circumstance and finds peace in the turmoil because she trusts. Her life may be in chaos, but her heart is calm and hopeful because of where she has her focus.

The God Girl is the best girl you can be. She is you when you accept Christ and yourself and when you want to be better but are happy with who you are. She is who you were meant to be, a child, deeply loved by a God who calls you his Girl. The God Girl is the essence of your soul. Take heart in your position and find hope in his love. You are a God Girl and you are God's.

God Girl Checklist

Pray about it—This week pray the same thing every day: "God, show me the sin in my life. And if the hard times I'm experiencing aren't because of sin, then show me that you are just pruning away the good to get to the best." Then listen. Listen each day. Study his Word and see what comes to you so you can determine what needs to be cut out of your life and why.

Concentration cards—Don't let your prayers get distracted. Practice concentration. That means constantly putting your thoughts back onto God, even though they wander. Don't get upset; just put them back on him when you feel a drift. To help with this, make concentration cards. Get some 3-by-5 cards and write out the things you want to pray about or concentrate on in your prayer time. Then keep them in front of you as you start to pray. Look at them often so you don't get off track and drift into thinking about the last fight you had with your friend or what you are going to do Friday night. Make a list like this: confess, adore, thank him, pray for Mom/Dad/BFF, etc. The concentration cards will keep you more focused than you will be if you just let your prayer wander.

My thank-you list—Wanna really thank God for everything? Then sit down and write a thank-you list. Think of everything, and I mean everything, that you are thankful for. The sun, the stars, your bed, your parents, your dog, Jesus, your church, the Bible, forgiveness, everything. Not just super-spiritual stuff but everything good. It all comes from him. Have you thanked him lately for it?

Create a verse list—A verse list is just a list of verses on a particular subject, kind of like a concordance. I started mine ten years ago, and I couldn't live without it. I go to it whenever I need help on a particular topic. It keeps me grounded in God's Word and helps me to memorize key verses that I want at my fingertips. Have you ever said, "Man, I wish I could remember that verse that was so good"? Well, this verse list will help you to keep those kinds of things close to your eyes and your heart. So here's how you make one: make a list of all the things you want to know about God and your life. Things like salvation, fear, love, sex, fighting, and so on. Then look up every verse you can find on it that connects with you. Write the verses down or type them up next to each topic. Then when you are looking for the verse that you need, you'll be able to find it quickly. You'll also be able to use your list for a devotional. Need help on worry today? Go to your list of verses on worry and read them all. A verse list is a great way to learn God's Word and find your way into it quickly.

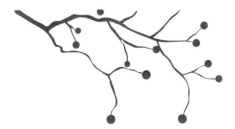

A Final Word to the God Girl

Being a God Girl is the most amazing and powerful thing you will ever be. When you decide that God's Word alone defines who you are and what you do, you find everything you need for life, hope and for peace. God defines the God Girl because she is his. God first, girl second. She belongs to him, serves him and loves him. To those who don't get it, you might seem out of touch with the world, but take heart, you aren't out of touch, you are just out of agreement. The world doesn't define the God Girl (that would be a "World Girl"). She doesn't take its ideas of good and bad and make them her own, but she examines everything she reads, hears, and sees through the light of God and his Word.

Being a God Girl will change you, every day. In everything you do, you will find more happiness and direction because your will, will be in line with His. Pastor James MacDonald puts it this way, "If your faith isn't changing you, it hasn't saved you." To a lot of people that sounds like bad news or heavy lifting. But to the God Girl that sounds like confirmation that her life is on the right track. When you are constantly improving, constantly agreeing with God that your way of thinking or acting is wrong and making the proper adjustments, you will see amazing changes in your life, your confidence, your peace, and your hope.

It is my prayer that none of this should overwhelm you but instead give you a sense of excitement and adventure. Even if you look at your life in disgust you should be encouraged, because those who are really the worst off are those who see nothing wrong with the sin in their lives. There is great strength to be found in calling sin, sin, and that strength is in the knowledge that all sin can be rejected not only by you but by the God who you have invited into your life. With help like that how can you lose? The presence of sin in your life just proves how much you need the God who saves. Be encouraged, my friend, and find the strength and hope to change not only your life with this information, but the lives of those around you as well.

Log on to www.ifuse.com to talk to more God Girls like yourself and to ask me questions. I look forward to seeing you there.

Hayley

Hayley DiMarco is founder of Hungry Planet, a company that creates cutting-edge books to connect with the multitasking mind-set. Hungry Planet is where she writes, co-writes, or edits all of the company's content for teens and former teens. She has written or co-written numerous bestselling and award-winning books, including *Dateable, Mean Girls, Sexy Girls, Technical Virgin, B4UD8,* and *The Woman of Mystery*. Hayley lives with her husband and daughter in Nashville, Tennessee.

You can find Hayley at www.ifuse.com and her books at www.hungryplanet.net

More Relevant Reads

from  Hungry Planet

Dating or waiting? Hungry Planet
tells you everything you need to know.

HAYLEY & MICHAEL DiMARCO

Hungry Planet challenges
teen guys to be men of God.

God Guy

Michael DiMarco

The Ultimate Bible just for the God Girl!

It's a blank canvas—design your own cover! Download patterns and stencils at GodGirl.com.

AVAILABLE IN
APRIL
2011

With special features like Ask Yourself, Prayers, God Girl Stories, and Know This Devotions, all written by bestselling author Hayley DiMarco, the *God Girl Bible* is a must-have for girls thirteen and up! If you're ready to grow closer to God, grow in your faith, and join an online group of girls from around the globe growing together, the *God Girl Bible* is for you.

Revell
a division of Baker Publishing Group
www.RevellBooks.com

Hungry Planet
www.hungryplanet.net

Available Wherever Books Are Sold